Gardens of the World

Two Thousand Years of Garden Design

Moulton
College

NORTHAMPTONSHIRE

Profit through Skill

JEAN-PAUL PIGEAT

Gardens of the World

Two Thousand Years of Garden Design

Translated from the French by Susan Pickford

Flammarion

Contents

© Archipel studio, 2003
An Archipel studio production
10, rue Louis-Bertrand — 94200 Ivry-sur-Seine

Editorial direction: Thomas Brisebarre

Editor: Juliette Neveux

Editorial assistant: Catherine Lucchesi

Picture research: Céline Quétier

Copy editor: Kathryn Lancaster

Simultaneously published
in French as *Jardins du Monde*
© Éditions Flammarion, 2003

English-language edition
© Éditions Flammarion, 2003
26, rue Racine
75006 Paris

03 04 05 4 3 2 1

ISBN: 2-0801-1272-4
N° d'édition: FC0428-03-IX
Dépôt légal: 09/2003

Printed in Italy

The art of gardens

I have been exploring the world's loveliest gardens for over thirty years now. I became interested in garden design almost by chance. To begin with, gardens and parks meant little more to me than a backdrop to the architecture I had come to study. But little by little, their magic took a hold of me. I visited dozens of gardens—large ones, small, intimate ones, famous ones, little-known but much-loved ones. People often ask me which I think are the loveliest gardens in the world. I always find it difficult to answer. Is it the best known, or one I discovered recently and which fired me with fresh enthusiasm? One thing is certain: this is a superb time for garden design. Every year, the Chaumont Garden Festival in France's Loire valley develops over 250 innovative garden design projects submitted by talented landscape architects from all over the world.

This book sets out to explore the history of garden design all over the world. Each chapter begins by examining a modern example of various classic types of garden design, because gardeners have always borrowed ideas from each other, adapting them to their own climes, sometimes with the most unexpected results.

The modern archetypes we examine illustrate the universal and timeless appeal of certain garden designs. Each chapter includes a visit to an internationally famous historical garden that illustrates the theme perfectly, and a discussion of the developments and innovations over the centuries. The analysis will drawn on references to other, less well known gardens. In total, this book features over one hundred gardens from all four corners of the globe. The most important gardens are highlighted in the text, while the key features of lesser gardens are explored in the illustrations and captions. This does not mean that we consider these gardens to be

somehow inferior—rather that their contribution to the history of garden design can be summed up in a few words.

Of course, the choice in any book of this sort is of necessity subjective. Some gardens have been left out, not because they were in any way less beautiful or enchanting than the others, but because another garden provided an equally good illustration of that particular style but had the advantage of being better known.

We are proud of the way historical gardens and the latest, most innovative designs stand side by side in this book. After all, an unexpected juxtaposition of styles is always the best way to spark new ideas. We hope this book will prove a source of inspiration for all gardening enthusiasts.

A terraced garden of strips of turf and rubber. Morat, Switzerland, 2002.

In the Beginning:
Water Gardens

Gardens cannot exist without water. Throughout history, power has been in the hands of whoever controlled the water supply. In the past, well-watered gardens were a way for princes and kings to display their power. By their lavish use of this precious resource for their own pleasure, to produce oases of greenery in the desert, they demonstrated their control over the very life of their subjects. The earliest gardens were little more than fenced-off stretches of land that contained a natural spring used to water trees, vegetables, and flowers. The local prince would come and visit once in a while to remind his subjects whom they had to thank for all this luxuriant vegetation. Oriental rulers often spent their time going from garden to garden as a means of displaying their status as ruler.

In a similar vein, many private companies today create gardens as a visible expression of their success. If money or water begin to run short, the garden—an expendable luxury—is the first cost to be reduced. This desire to produce a garden as physical proof of an individual's power—for only the powerful can afford to be wasteful of precious resources—was the reasoning behind the Cardinal d'Este's superb gardens on a hillside in Tivoli.

The history of gardens is intimately linked with the story of man's quest for an abundant and reliable water supply.

The Fountain of Life, fresco (1418–1430) by Giacomo Jaquiero (1403–1453). Detail of people bathing. Castello della Manta, Saluzzo, Italy.

Méry-sur-Oise

Pascal Cribier, Lionel Guibert, and Patrick Blanc, 1990, Méry-sur-Oise, France

The concrete channels and pools mimic the arabesques of classical gardens. The trees, trimmed perfectly round, are a modern version of the ancient art of topiary. The garden is a harmonious balance of tradition and modernity.

Méry-sur-Oise is a small commuter town in the suburbs of Paris. It is no different from the dozens of other similar towns that ring the French capital, except for the view of a famous bell-tower visible from the main road—the steeple of the church in the next town along, Auvers-sur-Oise, where Van Gogh lived the last few years of his life and where he is buried. On the marshy banks of the river Oise stands a château surrounded by a vast private garden. The château was once home to the Comtesse de Ségur, a nineteenth-century aristocrat remembered for her still popular books for children. The eighteenth-century building was recently restored with no expense spared by its latest owners, the French company Vivendi. The garden design was inspired by one of the multinational giant's most lucrative branches: the water industry.

It is relatively rare for major companies to become involved in such commissions, and the landscape architects who won the contract came up with one of the most unusual and innovative gardens to have been laid out in Europe for some years. The designers Pascal Cribier, Lionel Guibert, and Patrick Blanc chose to focus on "how water determines the appearance of a landscape and the style of vegetation through its presence, powerful or scarce, measured or whimsical. Wherever there is water, whether it gushes forth abundantly or trickles sparsely, plant life springs up. Following their own choice of path, through a vast meadow planted with willow copses, the visitors discover all the magic of water: rushing in cascades and mountain torrents, watering thirsty Busy Lizzies; the stagnant ponds typical of tropical climes, filled and refilled with warm rain that splashes over white water lilies; the frozen lakes of the far north, where arctic brambles sprawl over the ice; the brackish water of salt marshes where edible

samphire grows, covered with a thin silver membrane… The visit is designed as a learning experience illustrating the strategies used by the plants to survive in each of the different climates and environments. For the first time, water—the fundamental element of life—is the key to understanding the flora that flourishes in all climes, wherever water is present in some form."*

This water garden is striking in both its originality and its modernity. It is a worthy heir to the great traditions of the history of garden design. Like many great gardens of the past, it is a reflection of power. Yesterday's prince has given way to today's industrial magnate. And while the company president who commissioned the garden has since changed jobs, the garden remains a testament to his vision. It is a crystallization of all the latest scientific knowledge available at the time of its creation, just as the Hanging Gardens of Babylon displayed a mastery of irrigation and the fountains in the gardens of the Villa d'Este were designed to show off the latest techniques of water engineering.

Facing the château of Méry-sur-Oise are two asymmetrical rectangular ponds. The first is filled with green, flowing water, while the second, which is smaller, is filled with stagnant water and algae. This is a life-sized experiment in how plants live in water.

The first part of the visit explores how water is vital for plants. Walls built of volcanic stone illustrate varying degrees of water saturation: permanent dampness, oozing, trickling, or condensation. Further on, six more ponds with varying levels of water purity explain the process of how minerals leach into water. One pond filled with reverse osmosis water that gives off bubbles of gas is edged with catalpa trees trimmed perfectly round. The third part of the visit explores the effects of temperature on water and plant life. One zone presents plants that survive in temperatures permanently below freezing, while another has plants that live in tepid water.

Although the visit is relatively short, it is nonetheless as fascinating as a trip to Hellbrunn in Austria or to Versailles—especially since visitors

are free to explore the garden at their own pace. However, it is to be regretted that the financial difficulties faced by Vivendi, the company that commissioned the garden, mean that it is likely to be abandoned, and that even in the best of cases the far-sighted vision of this scientific garden will sadly not be fully developed. But many gardens throughout history have met the same fate, and after all, one might consider that the gardens of Méry-sur-Oise are all the more charming for being ephemeral.

* *Le Jardin de Méry-sur-Oise* (Paris: Vivendi Universal, 2000).

The Villa d'Este

Hippolyte d'Este, 1550, Tivoli, Italy

The intricacy and abundance of the water features at the Villa d'Este make this garden unmissable. The water is supplied by two aqueducts. While water was plentiful four hundred years ago, today the grounds often run short during the summer months.

The gardens at the Villa d'Este are an absolute reference in the history of garden design. Many visitors return time and time again, as enraptured by the profusion of the fountains as on their very first visit. Personally, I have been back seven or eight times, and on this latest occasion, I have brought some friends along with me. They are newcomers to the world of the historic garden, and I am looking forward to showing them round. It is late October, and the weather is cool. The entrance to the gardens, right in the heart of the village, is almost hidden, and the stone courtyard looks modest. The works that Hippolyte d'Este ordered in 1550 are still haunted by the ambience of the ruined convent that he transformed into this sumptuous villa. We enter the palace, straight into the reception hall. An enormous fresco painted by Gerolamo Muziano represents the villa and its gardens as they were originally planned. Although my friends do not yet know it, the fresco is a faithful representation of the villa and gardens that we are about to visit: both have survived practically untouched to the present.

Hippolyte d'Este was staying in Tivoli in autumn 1550, when he came across the old convent here, in a superb setting, overlooking the valley. He spent two months there, and enjoyed his time there so much that he decided to turn the convent into a villa and lay out some superb gardens.

We go out onto the first balcony for a glimpse of the gardens, the terraces descending in graceful tiers, and the fountains. My friends are struck dumb with amazement, and can't wait to go outside and explore. But they must be patient a little longer. The cardinal wanted his visitors to discover the garden from another perspective. They began at the bottom of the valley, from Via Tiburnia, and slowly wended their way up the hill, from terrace to terrace, symbolically submitting to the glory of the cardinal as they climbed upwards. Later, when we have walked down to the bottom of the hill, to the statue of the Ephesian Diana, we will rest for a while, then climb back up. It is much more interesting to approach the villa from the bottom of the hill.

Only by climbing the hill does the secret of the garden become fully apparent—the abundance of water, praised by awe-struck visitors for nearly five centuries. The water is taken from two aqueducts. The first, leading from the river Rivellese, also provides the village with drinking water. Beneath the interior courtyard of the palace lie three vast water tanks that feed some of the fountains. The second aqueduct takes water from the river Aniene to feed the Ovato fountain before flowing down to fill the fishponds and the lower reaches of the garden. When the level of the Aniene is high, the water flows at a rate of at least 317 gallons (1200 liters) per second. However, the river often runs almost dry in summer, and the gardeners are obliged to improvise with inelegant canvas-covered pipes.

The walk of a thousand water spouts is lined with sculptures covered in thick emerald moss. Experts believe that removing the moss would now damage the statues irreparably. The water organ, on the other hand, was recently fully restored. Parts of the original organ were taken from Hadrian's Villa.

Let's begin our visit the classic way, at the bottom of the hill. Four fountains are laid out round a ring of cypresses. In line with this ring of trees are two fountains made of heaps of rock, oozing with water, known as the Metae Sundantes (Latin for "sweating pillars"). They were built in imitation of a famous fountain that stood near the Coliseum in ancient Rome. In the same line there is also the Swan fountain. We walk as far as the three huge, rectangular fishponds and turn towards the Neptune fountain, then on to the Organ fountain, the highlight of this lower stretch of the garden. The impression of all of these fountains is one of a certain theatricality. The star of the show is indisputably the Organ, now lovingly restored to its former glory. During our visit, my friends and I were greeted by a musician who had

spent several hours repairing, then tuning the instrument and was delighted to hear the organ playing underwater once more as if by magic. To reach this terrace, we had to climb several long flights of steps, with fountains sending plumes of water high into the air on either side of us.

We continued climbing to reach the Ovato fountain and the grotto of Venus before walking on along the famous avenue of a hundred fountains, overgrown with moss on this late autumn day. At the far end, the Rome fountain awaits us. It is an idealized model of ancient Rome, while we gaze out at the panorama over the valley to the real Rome that lies below us. Only once we had reached this climactic moment did the Pandora fountain begin to play. We walked up the double flight of steps to explore the marvels of the villa itself.

Water gardens, past and present

The earliest archaeological traces of gardens date back to three thousand years B.C.E., in the city of Susa, in ancient Mesopotamia. These first gardens consisted of beds that were regularly spaced, both because it was more practical in terms of irrigation and as a visual reflection of the structure of Mesopotamian society. The garden fulfilled an important social role, functioning as a meeting place and a display of the city's wealth. Such early gardens were generally shaped like a cross, the most efficient way of distributing the water to all parts. Gardens were to be laid out as crosses for many centuries to come. Eventually, Islam conquered the Middle East and more and more palaces began to be built, frequently with a cross-shaped floor plan. Islamic towns and cities followed suit.

Sunken beds were dug at the central point of the cross, sometimes to depths of more than three feet (one meter), to protect the plants from the heat of the day. This also meant that the oranges and figs were within easy reach.

The Generalife in Granada ushered in a more modest style of garden. The princes were more sure of their grasp on power, and could thus afford to use water in a more playful, frivolous manner.

Supplying water to the ever-increasing population of Marrakech was a much more complicated issue. Enormous underground reservoirs were dug, following the example of other crowded cities like Baghdad or Tunis, and a complex irrigation system was installed to water the fruit and vegetables to feed the population. These are the ancestors of our modern underground water storage and supply systems. The aim has always been to protect the supplies from pollution and contamination.

The architects and planners who created the garden of Artas, near Bethlehem, were well aware of the symbolism of their act. The site they chose for the new garden, created in 2000, lay at the foot of the more than two-thousand-year-old reservoirs that supplied Jerusalem with water. Even though they were no longer in use, Solomon's pools were charged with significance. Creating a garden at the foot of the pools was a declaration of faith in the continuity of life.

Water was also used as a symbol of power in the early twentieth century in India, then still part of the British empire, when Edwin Lutyens

The abundant cascades of the Tanner fountain, in Portland, Oregon, is inspired by the region's magnificent natural scenery. Visitors can paddle in the pools and slide down the cascades.

was commissioned to come up with designs to reflect the role of the British viceroy. He drew on Mughal gardens, their abundant use of water in particular, in his plans for the capital in Delhi.

The water gardens at the Villa Lante and in Courances are much more intimate, created for the private pleasure of a bishop, a prince, or an ancient and noble family. In both of these cases, the garden is a symbol of the way the owners dominated the surrounding countryside and those who lived there.

In the twentieth century, Luis Barragan in Mexico and Fernando Caruncho saw water as the link between agriculture and gardening for pleasure, and staged gardens that were both recreational and functional. This was also the aim of the Tanner fountain, installed in Portland, Oregon, in 1970. It symbolizes wilderness, yet lies in the heart of the city, and thus brings a sense of identity that was somewhat lacking. The creative image of both city and state is now crystallized in this powerful fountain. Garden designers and architects have always used water as a way of expressing power—and the more lavish the design, the more powerful and prestigious the prince.

The Artas valley, near Bethlehem, was called *Hortus* (meaning garden) in Latin. This name recalls the ancient terraces of the Nativity at the foot of Solomon's pools—three gigantic reservoirs that supplied Jerusalem with water.

The Generalife Gardens
Designer unknown,
fourteenth century,
Granada, Spain

The palace in the Generalife
gardens is relatively modest.
The fourteenth-century rulers
who commissioned the gardens
came here to relax. The canal
that flows from the ground-
floor arcades is so perfect
that six centuries later, it was
recreated almost identically
for the new garden.

The Generalife gardens

Water has always been an important theme in the Generalife gardens in the Alhambra, Granada, Spain. Like the gardens of the Villa d'Este, the Generalife gardens are on a hillside and are blessed with an abundant spring, which makes all sorts of original water features possible. One of the most interesting, although it is rarely mentioned in books, is the water staircase which Andrea Navaggero described back in the sixteenth century as follows: "In a garden situated in the highest part of these sites, a broad staircase leads to an esplanade on which stands a rock, from which flows all the water used in the palace [...] The staircase is worked with consummate art. The steps are carved to receive the water, and the right-hand banister is hollowed out, forming a channel from top to bottom, and since at the top the cocks of each part are separate, they can be opened to make the water flow either down the banister, or pour over the steps themselves." It is extremely pleasant to dip one's hand in the channel in the banister as one walks down, and on each terrace, surrounded by a ring of dressed stones, a little fountain that draws from the same water refreshes the atmosphere.

Lower down the hill, the water collects in pools, in particular on the patio with the cypresses and the long basin which recently had a number of water jets installed. It is rather a shame, since the surface of the water no longer gives a smooth, unruffled reflection of the surrounding galleries. When I was visiting the Alhambra a few years ago, the system had broken down and I was able to see that the Belgian landscape architect René Pechère was perfectly right in saying that the new water jets are far from being an improvement. The Generalife is a more sophisticated, nobler, and more playful version of the great irrigated gardens found in the Middle East.

The Menara gardens, Marrakech

Marrakech has a surprise in store for the first-time visitor: the vast reaches of calm, smooth water in the *agdals* (olive groves), which contrast sharply with the foaming water rushing through the irrigation channels. Marrakech has numerous gardens, although it took the locals several centuries before they were fully assured of a regular water supply. There are no magical springs welling up from the ground; the water must be brought in from elsewhere. Among the many words for a garden used in Marrakech is the term *buhayra*, which refers directly to water, since it literally translates as large pool or small sea.

The great gardens of Marrakech are a vast orchard of fruit trees with a large pool providing water for irrigation. This style of irrigated garden is found all over the former Almohad empire, from Seville to Baghdad. As early as the twelfth century C.E., it was recognized that water was the most precious feature of the garden. When Islam spread to the north of Africa in the seventh century, the old gardens left behind by the Babylonians, Egyptians, and Persians were all destroyed. Their irrigation techniques were forgotten. Without adequate watering techniques, the new Islamic rulers could not hope to rival the magnificence of the botanical gardens of the Assyrians. Destroying the gardens was a way of crushing a symbol of the former royal power.

From the eighth century onwards, irrigation systems began to be dug once more, to water new towns where the housing was no longer kept separate from the gardens—forerunners of today's planned garden cities. Marrakech was extremely densely populated, and it became clear that the city would have to find new green spaces for the increasing number of inhabitants. The Menara gardens were laid out with a lake in the grounds, similar to gardens in Seville. The lakes were fed from naturally occurring underground water supplies or from streams from the nearby Atlas mountains. The underground reservoirs, called *khetarra*, stopped the water from evaporating before it could be used. They were so efficient that many have survived to the present day, although in very poor condition.

The princes made it a priority to provide gardens for the local population, where they could grow food as well as enjoy themselves. The Menara gardens in Marrakech were roughly the same size as the Medina, or market, giving an idea of their importance to the population. Nature, and especially water, were presented in an artificial setting: the lakes were perfectly rectangular, the park was dotted with pavilions, the irrigation system was not hidden away, and there were ramparts in place to protect the crops. Luxuriant vegetation grew side by side with farmed crops. The caliphs generously supported the public gardens as symbols of their power, but the inevitable consequence was that the gardens were neglected when they began to play a less significant political role.

It is no coincidence that the new sultans who chose to live in Marrakech in the nineteenth century set out to restore the Menara gardens, as was reported by the Moroccan historian An-Nâsirî: "It is a very large garden consisting

of several cultivated patches of land, distinguished by their borders, their names, and the labourers who are set to work there. Each patch has one or several sorts of trees growing olives, grenadines, apples, oranges, grapes, figs, walnuts, almonds, and other species. Each of these sorts of tree produces thousands of fruits every year. The orange harvest alone can be hugely profitable in a good year. Each patch also grows flowers, spices, and vegetables of various colours, flavors, scents, and other characteristics. There is an innumerable variety of these. Certain sorts are unknown in Morocco and come from other countries. In the middle of the garden are gigantic ponds on which boats and skiffs navigate. They are fed by the *khetarra*, which wind like rivers, irrigating the gardens and powering the numerous mills. There are ponds that measure some two hundred paces along each side. The gardens also contain pavilions worthy of the Persian kings, cupolas that are reminiscent of the Caesars, and resting places in the Omeyyad style. […] Altogether, this garden is a paradise on earth which is more beautiful than many places of recreation in Syria and Persia."*

* Quoted by Mohammed El Faïz in *Jardins de Marrakech* (Arles, Actes Sud, 2000).

The great pond in the Menara gardens in Marrakech is useful as well as elegant, as it is used as a reservoir. The guard house is decorated with *zellige* (earthenware mosaic), and is also as pretty as it is functional.

The Villa Lante

The Villa Lante has shades of both the Generalife, in the way water links a wild zone to a cultivated one, and the Villa d'Este, in the subtle and sophisticated way water is used. The gardens at the Villa Lante play with water in a highly theatrical manner, showing how water unites wild, uncultivated plains and mountains and the civilised world. Five successive levels tell the story: nature wild or tamed, savage or civilized, brutal or displaying the polished manners of the Renaissance.

In the upper reaches of the garden, water is drawn from various springs in the hills and flows through a sacred wood to the Fountain of the Flood. The muses watch over the garden from two pavilions that stand hidden amongst the trees. The water flows from the Dolphin fountain over a terrace and down some steps, forming a water staircase. The carved swirls of stone imitate ripples in the water, or possibly the back of a shrimp—the emblem of the Gambara family. It flows on down to the Giants' fountain and then along the canal that runs down the middle of the cardinal's table to refresh the guests. The next level down has several grottoes—the Grotto fountain, and the grottoes of Neptune and Venus. A few steps further on are the smaller villas, as well as the immense floral display and pyramidal fountain. We have gone from the rather gloomy upper levels to light airiness. A symbolic gate leads out to the village and the local inhabitants. The water flows on to a great pond where the locals could bring their horses to drink and wash them down. The Villa Lante has long been popular with visitors to the Rome region, and has inspired many other water gardens.

Courances

Courances
Designer unknown,
seventeenth century
(restored 1900–1907
by A. Duchêne),
Courances, France

Courances was long attributed
to André Le Nôtre, but
wrongly, it seems. However, it is
no less magnificent for that.
Today, the garden is strictly
classical, almost minimalist,
having been restored by the
current owners, who chose a
design inspired by agricultural
techniques to avoid vain,
fussy prettiness.
Above: A dolphin water spout.
Facing page: The garden
in winter.

Courances also has a tale to tell about the
shared history of water and gardens. Courances
has thirteen springs that feed the ponds, and
the abundance of water means that the atmosphere is deliciously cool. Monsieur Dulaure
was probably thinking of the machines that
powered the fountains in Versailles when he
wrote: "[In Courances] it is a natural effect for
the water to flow constantly, unlike certain
grandiose cascades that seem to live from one
moment to the next only with great effort, and
then must rest, like a painting that could disappear and leave the frame empty."

The river Ecole runs through the park. Its
waters, drawn from the springs, feed the ponds
through underground pipes, all the way to the
far end of the park. The ground slopes gently,
and the water flows smoothy and unruffled. The
château itself is built on an island, and visitors
must pass between two canals to reach it. On
the far side of the château, the smooth surface
of the water, like a mirror, draws the gaze down
to the distant view of the village of Moigny.

Alongside the château is a horseshoe-shaped
pond dominated by a statue of Arethusa with
two dolphins that pour water into the pond. The
most charming spot in the whole park is the
place where the three walks meet, with a view of
the lake on one side and the canal on the other.
Nearby is a row of stepped cascades sheltered by
dignified old trees, where the water flows gently

over the terraces and splashes over the levels. There are no bright, garish colors in Courances, only the green of the trees and lawns, the grey-blue of the water, and the reflections of the clouds. These muted tones are the result of a deliberate decision by the current owners to give the garden a strikingly modern atmosphere. The passing centuries have left little trace here.

The garden of Courances is sometimes wrongly attributed to the great French gardener Le Nôtre. In fact, it dates from before his time. However, it does boast a number of features that are characteristic of the great gardener's work: symmetrical flowerbeds, a lake, features designed to catch the reflection of the clouds, twin canals, and rows of statues. Here, despite the modern atmosphere, time seems to stand still. Horses gambol in the meadows; the only reminder of the twenty-first century is the distant hum of farm machinery.

The Barragan water gardens

Luis Barragan participated in
a number of major city
development works in Mexico
City in the 1960s. He was
unparalleled in his use of vivid
colors juxtaposed with expanses
of water, drawing both on
traditional Mexican art forms and
a very modern sense of space.
Above: Los Clubes.
Facing page: Las Arboledas.

The Barragan water gardens, like the Agdal in
Marrakech, combine pleasure and utility. Luis
Barragan was a Mexican architect. His work
has never received widespread public attention, although he designed several exceptional
water gardens in the 1960s. Most of these were
designed as part of upmarket building projects
for housing or leisure facilities. Water is a
precious commodity in Mexico, and so Luis
Barragan planned ponds or channels in the
shade of tall trees. In Las Arboledas, a long
black canal runs alongside an avenue of eucalyptus trees before stopping short at the foot
of a bright blue wall. In Los Clubes, a number
of ponds and cascades lie round walls painted
a warm sienna brown. These high walls
painted in strong colors form the base of
Barragan's original architectural vocabulary,
which seems to draw on traditional Arabic
architecture but with its own pronounced leaning towards modernity. The strict lines of
Barragan's water gardens call the Agdal in
Marrakech irresistibly to mind.

The Caruncho water gardens

Fernando Caruncho's water gardens are at once traditional and yet extremely modern. Caruncho is widely held in Spain to be the most talented landscape architect of his generation. He uses strict combinations of traditional elements to come up with highly innovative designs. The garden he created in S'Arago in Catalonia,

for example, draws on the Arab-Andalusian tradition. The square ponds form patterns reminiscent of the Myrtle Courtyard in the Alhambra in Granada. They lead up to two summer pavilions with trellis walls covered in climbing plants. In Ollauri, Caruncho came up with a design for two ponds with a cypress planted in the center, a reference to classical Italian garden design,

reinterpreted with a modern twist. The functional-looking brick-lined ponds in Mas de les Voltes lie side by side with two large banks of wheat. The simplicity of the rural world and the sophistication of modern society join forces to stunning effect, just as they did in sixteenth-century gardens in Venice, or—to take a more modern reference—the gardens of Courances.

The S'Arago garden, 1987–1989, S'Arago, Costa Brava
Ollauri garden, 1985–1987, Ollauri, La Rioja
Mas de les Voltes garden, 1995–1997, Castel de Ampurdán
Fernando Caruncho, Spain

Caruncho's gardens use water like mirrors, reflecting the expanse of the sea and the sky.

Gardens of the Gods

At first glance, there might seem to be nothing in common between a Land Art creation designed to attract lightning strikes and the gardens at Versailles, separated by three hundred years of history. Yet, each in their own way, both tell the same story.

Gardens have always been a corner of paradise on earth—a way of trying to create an ideal world. It is hardly surprising, then, that so many gardens refer in one way or another to the gods of various mythologies. When the artist Walter de Maria set out to attract lightning in the great plains of the United States, he was, in a sense, playing God, calling the divine fire down to earth. In Bomarzo, visitors can enter the subterranean realm of the gods via the mouth of a monster sculpted directly in the rock.

Walter de Maria is not the only artist to have found inspiration in this confrontation of man against the forces of nature. Painters, sculptors, and musicians have often drawn on similar symbolic rivalries. Louis XIV, the Sun King, measured himself against God by planning the palace and magnificent gardens at Versailles. Such symbolic confrontations with the gods are still relevant today in understanding recent developments in garden design.

Many contemporary paintings of Versailles deliberately exaggerated the size of the palace and grounds as a way of flattering the king's desire to dominate nature. They show avenues stretching almost to the horizon and vast plains waiting to be turned into elegant lawns—all to the glory of the Sun King. Pierre Patel, *View of the Gardens and Palace of Versailles from the Avenue de Paris*, 1668, Château de Versailles, France.

The Lightning Field

Walter de Maria, 1974, near Quemado, New Mexico, USA

It is a terrifying and humbling experience to be caught in a thunderstorm in open country. Blinding lightning flashes split the sky while the thunder cracks overhead. It is tempting to try and shelter under a tree, but some primeval instinct warns us this safe haven is the most dangerous spot in a storm. This is the emotion that the Lightning Field seeks to recreate.

Walter de Maria's original idea, back in 1974, was to create a work of Land Art that would be truly sublime, giving a violent, primitive, abstract vision of the landscape. The chosen site was to be near Quemado, New Mexico. It is located in the heart of an extremely flat plain surrounded by low-lying hills, several miles distant. The site gives a disturbing impression of shutting the visitor in, so that he can never escape the endless expanse of land and sky and the light that floods the plain.

The work of art itself consists of hundreds of steel poles planted at regular intervals over an area measuring roughly 1 km by 1.6 km. The light in the middle of the plain is so intense that the poles can hardly be seen at midday. They only become clearly visible towards evening, when the sun is low on the horizon. The poles act as conductors and attract lightning. The work of art comes to life on stormy nights, when the poles draw down spectacular bolts of lightning, sometimes for minutes at a time. It is an extraordinary, exhilarating sight, giving a feeling of being in touch with terrifyingly powerful, superior forces. In its play of contrasts between dark and light, de Maria's work draws on the same artistic techniques as certain paintings by Claude Lorrain (1600–1682). It is also reminiscent of some eerie, melancholic landscapes by Caspar David Friedrich (1774–1840).

Watching the lightning play among the metal poles of Walter de Maria's installation is terrifyingly impressive. It is an almost Biblical visitation on this desert plain.

Versailles

André Le Nôtre, seventeenth century, Versailles, France

There are sculptures everywhere you look in Versailles, in gilded bronze and white or colored marble. The pictures show one of the lakes and the Latone fountain.

Bow down and tremble with fear, for you are to face the Sun King. Louis XIV was a living god—a fiery star at the center of a complex cosmogony. Versailles is the physical representation of the Sun King's boundless powers.

When the king first decided to build a magnificent palace in the heart of the mosquito-plagued plains to the west of Paris, the site seemed an odd choice. As the years passed and the costs of the immensely ambitious project rose ever higher, it seemed positively eccentric. Yet Louis XIV had a master plan: to force even nature to yield to his own divine power.

The layout of the gardens was an integral part of the king's master plan. Versailles was to be a reflection of his royal power. The château was to be the focal point, the sun round which the lesser stars of the court revolved. Even the view from the palace itself had to be carefully planned, especially towards the west where the sun set. The use the land was put to—agriculture and forestry—reflected the economic priorities of the day, as well as the state of contemporary scientific thought: "the discovery of new lands, the now complete vision of the universe, and major advances in science meant the men of this century had a more rational understanding of the work of the Creator. Nature, until then something to be feared, seemed finally to have revealed the secrets of all of its mechanisms. It was now up to men, and by right to the most powerful, to domesticate it for his own good, so that he could become a new demiurge and equal of the gods." *

Starting in 1661, work proceeded apace. The domain was extended further to the north and south, then to the west, where the marshlands were drained. The land to the south was flattened, while the slope to the north was extended. Festivities were organised to celebrate the cult of the Sun King: the Pleasures of the Enchanted Isle in 1664, and others to commemorate the signing of the treaty of Aachen in 1668. Dozens of other similar occasions followed, each a means to force the masons' hands, speed up the building works, and test some new technique or decoration. The Sun King could not be kept waiting; nor could he be seen to be lacking in imagination to create his own world.

"The sun brings order to the cosmos and dictates its own inflexible rules. But Apollo is also the god of harmony, bringer of peace, patron of the

arts and sciences. These in turn become instruments of royal propaganda and an ideological point of view imposed on nature, while the garden, the concrete representation of this, becomes the seat of absolute power and the favored instrument for glorifying the sovereign… Nothing can resist the will of the monarch turned god."*

However, the building works at Versailles were far from straightforward. The great marshes of the Gally plain were only dried by means of the huge pond dug along the grand canal. The marshlands to the south were likewise dried out by the creation of the Swiss pond. Elsewhere in the grounds, there was not enough water to feed the majestic fountains the Sun King dreamed of creating. The pond in Clagny was converted into a reservoir, surrounded with windmills to pump the water. Some miles away, in Bougival, a fiendishly clever machine was installed to transfer water from the Seine to an aqueduct that led straight to Versailles. On the plain, water was drawn from a chain of ponds by a network of canals and aqueducts over a distance of dozens of miles. The king even came up with a megalomaniac plan to pump water from the river Eure, and drew up a scheme that called on the services

of the military—infantry battalions and squadrons of dragoons. The idea was a complete failure. The only part to be built was part of an aqueduct, rapidly abandoned, opposite the château de Maintenon, home to the king's secret new bride. Symbolically, this ruined aqueduct represented the king's fall from divine grace. From then on, he could only play at being god in his palace at Versailles, turning on the fountains one by one as the water supply dictated.

Louis XIV managed to defeat time by uprooting thousands of fully grown trees and bringing them from great distances to plant instant

forests, at the cost of the lives of hundreds of laborers. He also set out to create a vegetable garden that would bring forth produce as he, and not the seasons or climate, dictated, and twisted the trees into strange and unnatural shapes. He brought together animals from all over the world in his own private menagerie, recreating Noah's ark. His numerous illegitimate children were symbolized in the gardens as angels and cherubs. Louis XIV ruled by divine right, and was the equal of God on earth.

* Pierre-André Laublade. *Les Jardins de Versailles* (Paris, Scala, 1995).

The view from the terrace towards the Orangery and the Swiss pond. The smooth surface of the water contrasts sharply with the elegant patterns of the exotic plants. The view is designed to impress the visitor with the monarch's great wealth and power, as displayed in his extensive botanical collections and the skill of his engineers.

Paradise gardens

Isola Bella, jutting into Lake Maggiore like the prow of a ship, is dedicated to the beauty of a princess. The island became an idyllic haven in 1620 thanks to the efforts of Prince Vitaliano Borromeo. It took thousands of tons of rocks and soil to build the ten terraced tiers that rise 105 feet (32 meters) above the lake.

Nature has held a supernatural fascination for mankind since the dawn of time. The gods have always been attributed outstanding natural sites, such as Mount Olympus or Machu Picchu in the Andes. Temples were built in these holy places as manifestations of the divine power on earth. Other unusual or awe-inspiring natural features were also seen as propitious for communicating with the gods. Mountains were the closest man would get to the skies, and chasms and caves—especially underwater—were the mouths of hell. Over the centuries, the symbolism of such spiritual sites began to be incorporated into gardens. In Bomarzo, for example, the grounds of the Villa Orsini are thronged with monsters and mythological creatures, statues scattered in the sacred wood, where pagan deities roam. Gardens play a major role in the history of Christianity, from the garden of Eden to the garden of Gethsemane. Convents and monasteries were often built on inaccessible mountainsides, as in Greece, and their gardens were conducive to the contemplative life. Some gardens, such as Bom Jesus de Braga in Portugal, had a staircase on a hillside so that visitors could climb up to heaven, while the numerous fountains in others often refer to miraculous, life-giving springs that nestle in shady valleys.

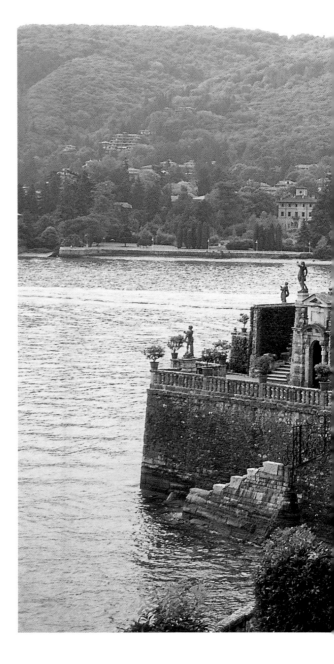

Garden symbolism is not confined to Christianity. The perpendicular canals in traditional Islamic gardens represent the universe and the four points of the compass. And, as in the Christian religion, verandas open to the sky symbolized free and open communion with Allah. In Cordoba, the

orchard of ancient trees round the mosque is one of the earliest surviving examples. In Japan, Zen Buddhist gardens were also places of meditation and dialogue with the spiritual world. A garden consisting of a few rocks on raked sand was a focal point allowing the monks to free their spirits to soar throughout the universe. Sometimes, men of great power tried to rival the gods, re-shaping the earth as in Isola Bella on Lake Maggiore in Italy, creating gardens and palaces of vainglorious extravagance that have survived while the bones of their founders have since crumbled into dust.

Gods and nature in the ancient world

For the ancient Greeks, the gods were physically present in the landscape. Nature, gardens, and the cycle of life were inextricably linked, and the land was a key element of their culture and their relationship with the gods and with life itself. The great archaeological sites of ancient Greece, such as Olympus, Epidaurus, Ephesus, and the Parthenon, reflect this exceptional bond with the stunning Greek landscape which gave them divine protection. The first glimpse of the Olympic stadium after arriving through the tunnel, for example, is truly breathtaking in its sheer symmetry (seen from a slightly diagonal angle), with the gently sloping banks, and the calm of the surrounding hills.

Delos still bears the traces of this association of the gods with the land. The land was under the protection of the gods, so by placing man at the heart of the landscape, his well-being was assured. Such religious beliefs were carried over

In ancient Greece, the poets preferred the countryside to tame gardens. To live in harmony with the landscape meant to be at peace with the gods. In sites such as the Parthenon, the stadium at Olympus that opens to the hills, or the cultivated groves on the hillsides, the landscape is full of symbolism.

into ancient Rome. The site at Preneste (now Palestrina) attests to the bond between the deities and nature, here in the shape of an immense temple that once covered the hillside. Many gardens housed grottoes that were considered entrances to the underworld, symbolizing the link between the land and the gods. Mouths sculpted in the rock round the entrances to such grottoes can be seen, for example, in Bomarzo and the Villa Aldobrandini in Frascati.

Bomarzo: The sacred wood

Bomarzo is a sacred wood, home to both good and evil spirits. The garden was commissioned by one of the Orsini princes, and designed by Pirro Ligorio. It is not known why there are so many works depicting monsters and other mythological and curious creatures here—sphinxes, giants, turtles, elephants, dogs, Neptune, Venus, Proserpine, a perilously tilting house, an open-air theater, a group of nymphs, a temple, a dragon, and an ogre, together forming a mysterious, initiatory path. The combination of the bizarre and phantasmagorical seem to be designed to transmit some kind of divine secret. There is no overriding plan—in fact, the ruling principle seems to be to throw the visitor off balance—literally in the case of the tilting house, where the senses are deliberately thrown off kilter, the perspectives distorted, and nature itself denatured. In the words of Ehrenfried Kluckert, "The garden of the Villa Orsini in Bomarzo cannot be compared to any other. It includes elements of the Renaissance, deforming their scale, and artistic products represented in an exaggerated and illusionistic manner. Likewise, we can only compare Bomarzo to the baroque gardens that were to come later if we think of it as decentralised and put into some kind of order, in a great park. But then the garden of Bomarzo would lose its identity." *

* Ehrenfried Kluckert. *Parcs et jardins en Europe* (Cologne, Könemann, 2000).

Mont Saint Michel and Christian gardens

Above: The magnificent double stairs in Bom Jesus de Braga.
Right: A majolica column in the convent of Santa Chiara.
Facing page: A walled garden in Mont Saint Michel.

The cloister gardens to be found in many European monasteries are places designed to be conducive to prayer, bringing the monks closer to God. They are symbolically left open to the sky. The famous monastery island of Mont Saint Michel, in France, seems to reach for the heavens. All the buildings lead ever higher up to the cloister right at the top of the hill, as close to God as it was possible to be.

The garden at Castelo do Bom Jesus, Braga in Portugal is a huge double set of stairs, flanked on either side by an oak wood. It was planned in the late eighteenth century by the architect Amarante. The turns of the staircase are decorated with rather pagan-looking statues. The staircase as a whole was designed to give access to the sanctuary at the top where men could enter into contact with God. It is a pleasant climb. There is water everywhere, but the real highlight of the climb is at its best in early spring: the banks of camellias, rhododendrons, and mimosa which shower visitors with fragrance. The steep slope is somewhat of a test of their religious devotion.

Another fine example is Santa Chiara in Naples, right in the heart of the city. Here, again, God shows his benevolence. The cloister of the convent of the Poor Clares was designed around a series of octagonal majolica columns, decorated with fruit and flower motifs entwined round them. The impression is one of tranquillity. The columns are very pale blue in color, which is easier on the eye under the harsh Neapolitan sun than blinding white would be. Between the columns are placed a number of benches decorated with scenes of daily life in centuries past. The light wood rafters trail vines. The atmosphere of this refined cloister is joyous, although the order of Poor Clares was, in theory at least, extremely strict.

The gardens of the Cordoba mosque

The gardens of the Cordoba mosque are especially interesting, as they survived the Catholic reformation of the zealous emperor Charles V unscathed. The mosque itself was not so fortunate: Charles' architects did not hesitate to destroy its colonnades to establish a cathedral on the same spot. For whatever reason, they left the trees standing. The gardens of the Cordoba mosque are an excellent example of traditional Arabic garden design: the rows of perfectly aligned trees are ringed with great circles of stone, which are linked by irrigation channels. I was fortunate enough to visit the Cordoba mosque on a day when it was raining heavily. The water poured out of the mosque's gutters and began to trickle, then gush through the irrigation channels. It was magical to watch the earth beginning to drink it in and exhale all sorts of wonderful, fresh, damp odors. It was like being in some primeval jungle.

Ryoan-ji

Ryoan-ji has become something of a cliché in terms of garden design—but as is often the way with clichés, it would be simply unthinkable not to include it. Since 1499, these fifteen stones placed in three groups on raked white sand have been a source of fascination for millions of people from all over the world. The first group has only three stones; the second five. The third group of seven forms a complex cabalistic sign of yin and yang. The rhythm of the garden is set by these numbers and by these stones laid out so that they cannot all be seen at once, in reference to the vastness of the universe that cannot be grasped by the mind of man. There can be no place more conducive to meditative contemplation in the world.

Ryoan-ji
Designed by Soami, based on an idea by Ozokawa Mazamoto, sixteenth century, Kyoto, Japan

Two contrasting visions of Ryoan-ji: the famous zen garden with its artfully positioned rocks, and a shady pine garden—an invitation to tranquil meditation.

Gardens as Expressions of Wealth

It is most instructive to compare past and present in terms of gardens. In the past, they were concrete expressions of the local ruler's power. For example, he was able to control the springs and thus the water supply to his subjects. By using large stretches of fertile land and lavishing huge sums of money on frivolous gardens, princes strove to be the equals of the gods. Above all, they wanted to outdo rival rulers in terms of ostentatious expenditure. This has been true throughout history. In more recent centuries, after the fall of the traditional feudal aristocracy in Western Europe, the garden as a display of wealth and source of prestige was kept up by the new ruling class—the bourgeoisie. Today, the new rulers who commission the most extravagant garden designs are multinational companies eager to acquire a cultural gloss for their financial glory.

Schönbrunn was built as a testimony to the might of the Habsburg dynasty. The palace gardens, vast stables, lawns, botanical collections, and menagerie were designed to rival the glory of Versailles.
Bernardo Bellotto, *The Palace and Gardens at Schönbrunn*, 1759–1761. Kunsthistorisches Museum, Vienna, Austria.

PepsiCo

Russell Page, 1981, Purchase, New York, USA

It might seem paradoxical, if not downright provocative, to begin with this garden. Yet the reasons for its creation have much in common with the ostentatious show gardens of the seventeenth and eighteenth centuries. In 1965, the Pepsi company decided to move from its New York headquarters to a site some thirty-five miles to the north, in Purchase. The new headquarters were built in grounds of about one hundred twenty five acres (fifty hectares), but the landscape needed improving. Over the years, the company has acquired some fifty contemporary sculptures for display, all extremely large, as a way of signifying the company's prosperity. To this end, the collection obviously had to be presented in a most striking way. In 1981, Pepsi called on the services of the great landscape architect Russell Page, who was then in the twilight of his career. His design was an absolute masterpiece.

He had to work with a very ordinary landscape and some extraordinarily powerful sculptures. He came up with a plan for a dialogue as a link between the individual pieces. In his book *Education of a Gardener,* * he told how he first of all looked at the relationships between the various elements of the landscape, whether a corner of a forest, a pond, a rock, a plant, or a flowerbed. He firmly believed that each gave off its own unique vibrations, depending on its

nature, colour, texture, or shape. The feel of a piece of marble, say, was different from that of sandstone or granite.

A golden path runs throughout the park and the plantations, ringing the sculptures and including them in the landscape as a whole. Smaller areas have their own hidden surprises, such as an azalea garden, an ornamental grasses garden, and a water garden of three rectangular ponds, where the water laps over onto the lawns. The atmosphere of the park is majestic and extremely refined. It easily holds its own against the best-known historical gardens. As Russell Page wrote, he used trees as sculptures and sculptures as flowers. He used everything that came to hand, and the result was superb harmony. **

* Harmondsworth: Penguin, 1985.

** See Marina Schinz, and Gabrielle van Zuylen,
   Les Jardins de Russell Page (Paris: Flammarion, 1992).

A giant trowel by Claes Oldenburg, a sculpture by Max Ernst, and elegant water features (following double spread) reveal the image PepsiCo wants to create: a prosperous company that supports the arts.

The Taj Mahal

Shah Jahan, 1632–1654, Agra, India

The story of the Taj Mahal has become such a byword for undying love that it seems almost churlish to include it in a section on displays of power. Yet only the most powerful of emperors could afford to build such a monument to his lost love—for the Taj Mahal is, in fact, a magnificently elaborate tomb.

In 1631, the empress Mumtaz Mahal died in childbirth. Her husband, the emperor Shah Jahan, was inconsolable and decided to build such a mausoleum as the world had never seen as a paean to the beauty of his late wife. The tomb itself, which faces south, is made entirely of white marble. It is surmounted by a gigantic cupola and framed by four minarets. Flanking the mausoleum are two stretches of lawn with square ponds in the center and, beyond them, two red sandstone mosques. The gardens are in front of the mausoleum. They are framed by two canals that cross, forming four squares, each of which is further subdivided into four. At the point where the canals meet, there is a square pond which reflects the mausoleum, just as in Vaux-le-Vicomte, where the château is mirrored in the square pool. As Germain Bazin wrote, "The presence of this immense 'paradise' in front of the funeral monument is obviously deliberate. A monumental gate leads into the garden. Was there ever a more elegant architectural design? Built to perpetuate the beauty of a mortal woman, its ethereal character has made her name live for ever." *

* Germain Bazin, *Paradeisos* (Paris: Chêne, 1988).

Gardens of power

The Book of Genesis tells us how God made man in his own image. In fact, the reverse is closer to the truth. Kings and conquerors have always called on their gods to give their actions divine legitimacy. Extravagant, ostentatious gardens were simply another way of displaying the power that the deities had bestowed upon them. Small wonder that monarchs and the powerful nobility sought to fill their gardens with symbolic references to their own divine glory.

Today, and in particular over the last twenty years, such ostentatious displays of wealth have no longer been the work of kings, but of the new aristocracy—the directors of multinational companies, who see a garden as a means of flaunting not only their financial health, but to their status as benefactors of society. These are the new patrons of the arts and culture. The PepsiCo garden in Purchase, near New York, is an excellent example.

The Taj Mahal—a tomb for a lost wife—is a great symbol of enduring love, but the building naturally reflects the wealth and status of the Shah who commissioned it. The gardens at Isola Bella were planned for similar reasons, as a homage to a beautiful princess, but they are much more intimate.

Gardens designed to flaunt the wealth and power of the owner are often not the most pleasant places to visit, as their sheer size and splendor are frequently simply overwhelming. Much more charming are the more intimate gardens, often with more complex designs with hedges and banks dividing the grounds into manageably sized units, such as the Alcazar in Seville. The juxtaposition of styles and influences gives the visitor a chance to broaden his horizons, learn about new plants, and admire the skill of the gardeners. Such gardens can be a sheer enchantment.

But the desire to draw attention to a newly acquired elevated social position often proved more alluring than such subtle pleasures. Nicolas Fouquet paid dearly for daring to outshine the king with his gardens at Vaux-le-Vicomte—but nevertheless he launched a fashion, and without his flamboyant gardens, Versailles, Peterhof, and

a host of other classical European gardens would never have seen the light of day. In the eighteenth century, the Age of Enlightenment, it seemed less important to put on such grandiloquent displays. The fashion was for more intimate gardens, such as Sanssouci and Queluz. Only the Habsburgs in Schönbrunn and the Bourbons of Naples in Caserte still indulged in homages to their own glory.

The aristocracy followed suit, preferring a more intimate style of garden. The Villa Garzoni was set in a bucolic valley, and part of the grounds were given over to woodlands where the Garzoni family could flirt and frolic with their guests. It is

likewise interesting to compare the pomp of Versailles to the relative modesty of Chatsworth.

In the twentieth century, gardens became more democratic, but were often still seen as a source of prestige. Original and innovative designs were a tourist attraction, and thus a boost to the reputation of the town or city that commissioned them. Many cities around the world have invested in gardens and garden festivals as a means of improving their image. Over the last twenty years, for example, the city of Paris has invested heavily in several garden projects involving internationally respected landscape architects.

This king handing his queen a charter in the grounds of the Alcazar in Seville is a noble image of royal power. It is a modern addition, and though it is somewhat lacking in finesse, it is typical of the statues found in public parks all over the world.

Gardens of the Alcazar in Seville

The gardens of the Alcazar in Seville are characterized not by death, but by the endless cycle of life. Their infinite charm is the result of their harmonious development over the centuries. From the days of the Arab princes back when Spain was an outpost of the Islamic empire to the present, every era has added a new garden, a new vision, extended the grounds, or created a new link between parts of the domain. The earliest gardens, created around the palace by the Arab rulers, were not destroyed when the Catholic kings took back their lost territory. On the contrary: they kept on the Arab gardeners to extend the gardens in the same style. Charles V commissioned a pavilion with a refreshing fountain in the center of the room in a typical Mudejar style. The former ramparts, converted into a belvedere, are difficult to date. Was the fishpond converted into a decorative fountain only in the eighteenth century? Were the gardens ornamented with blue and white tiles really laid out in the early twentieth century, despite their striking resemblance to Persian gardens? The sunken flowerbeds that look like dry ponds are a tradition dating back six centuries. There is even a typical English garden and maze, perfectly integrated into the overall scheme. The gardens of the Alcazar in Seville illustrate four great periods of garden design that meld harmoniously in a spirit of mutual understanding. A comparable architectural example of harmoniously combined styles would be the town of Palermo in Sicily.

Vaux-le-Vicomte

Vaux-le-Vicomte
André le Nôtre, 1656–1661,
Vaux-le-Vicomte, France

Walks stretching almost to the
horizon, topiary hedges, copses,
grottoes, lawns, unruffled
ponds and plashing fountains—
the first garden to have been
designed in the French style is
absolutely typical of the genre.

Vaux-le-Vicomte is deliberately, unambiguously ostentatious. It was built for Nicolas Fouquet, Inspector of Finance for Louis XIV, who wanted the most lavish of gardens. It was the first to reach such heights of extravagance. The château is set in a range of low hills. Le Nôtre drew inspiration from these surroundings to create a remarkable park where there is a surprise round every corner. Many authors have commented on the generous vistas and avenues that in fact make Vaux-le-Vicomte too grandiose to be really pleasant to walk round. The pleasure of a visit here is intellectual rather than sensual. The broad avenue leads the gaze all the way to the horizon and deepens the perspective. The two elaborate flowerbeds near the château form a transition between the highly decorative interiors and the open spaces of the park. The vista and the two ponds are framed by copses. Seen from the far side of the square pond, the château is exactly mirrored in its smooth waters. Walking a little further, the visitor is taken by surprise by the great canal and the fountain decorated with statues of nymphs on a lower level. The gaze is then drawn inexorably up to the top of the hill, on which stands the huge statue of the Farnese Hercules.

The extravagance of Vaux-le-Vicomte could not help but attract the wrath of Louis XIV when he came to visit his inspector of finance. The king was so jealous of this challenge to his divine power that he ordered the palace of Versailles to be built to overshadow this upstart. Vaux-le-Vicomte can thus be said to be the origin of the French fashion for impressively ostentatious gardens.

From Het Loo to Peterhof

Het Loo
Daniel Marot, 1685,
Apeldoorn, Netherlands

Peterhof
Jean-Baptiste Alexandre Le Blond,
1716, Saint Petersburg, Russia

The architects of the cascade lined with golden statues in Peterhof (above) and the intricate latticework of Het Loo (facing page) had the same inspiration—ostentatious displays of power and taste. The gardens are stages for the prince and his courtiers to strut on.

When Peter the Great decided to build the palace of Peterhof in 1714, he set out to rival Versailles. He chose a site of exceptional beauty, on a natural terrace overlooking the gulf of Finland. The garden was to be on two levels: the upper garden and the lower park. The large number of springs on the grounds meant that plenty of water features could be installed. On the upper level near the palace is Neptune's fountain, with its extraordinary collection of gilded bronze figures. In front of the palace is the Samson fountain and the water theater, a spectacle of fountains and cascades laid out to suggest an amphitheater. These feed the canal, which flows down over a distance of nine hundred eighty-four feet (three hundred meters) to the shore, where a pier juts out into the gulf. Two water staircases, each with seven levels, frame a grotto. The water flows progressively more smoothly along the canal, framed by twenty-two spouts. The furthest corners of the park are not forgotten: the grounds are home to 173 fountains in total. Some are dedicated to Neptune, Adam and Eve, and Triton. Others with names like the Tulip, the Umbrella, and the Bench, catch the visitor unawares, showering him with spray, following the example of traditional Italian Renaissance gardens. One fountain even has glass bells rung by the splashing water. The pavilions that line the beach have French names, such as Monplaisir, Marli, L'Ermitage, or l'Orangerie. Peter the Great was a fervent admirer of all things French, Versailles in particular, and his wish was to create in Peterhof a palace and grounds that would not only draw attention to his power, but also demonstrate that he was an enlightened monarch. In fact, Peterhof draws on Italian sources for inspiration as much as it does on Versailles. Its vista out over the sea gives it an open perspective unequalled anywhere else in Europe.

Het Loo may be smaller than Peterhof, but it is by no means less ambitious. In the late seventeenth century, the princes of Batavia had immense power, and their influence was felt all over the world. The garden is more modest, in line with the Puritan tastes of the Batavian princes, who scorned the ostentatious style typical of the Russian court. The gardens of Het Loo, planned in 1685 by Daniel Marot, imitated the gardens of Louis XIV. Its recent restoration in 1978 was carried out with the seventeenth-century French style very much in mind: a central avenue, flowerbeds designed to resemble embroidery, colonnades, statues, vases, latticework bowers, and topiary. Every detail was designed to ensure the court could not but acknowledge the prince's power, the superiority of his taste, and the sheer vastness of his domains.

Sanssouci

After the sheer extravagance of Peterhof, the palace Sanssouci denotes a return to a (relatively) reasonable size. The rulers of Prussia had several palaces in Potsdam, just outside Berlin, in a vast park. Sanssouci is a fairly long walk from the main royal residence, the New Palace. Built perpendicular to the New Palace, Sanssouci faces due south, and its sunflower yellow walls glow in the morning sun. The palace is relatively modest, having no upper stories. The central cupola and large wings are reminiscent of Vaux-le-Vicomte, on a much smaller scale, but just as elegant. The palace stands at the top of a series of six terraces on which vines and figs are cultivated. The plants are protected from the cold in winter by greenhouses built into the retaining terrace walls, with glass doors that can be opened in summer.

Sanssouci was very obviously designed as a symbol of wealth and power, but it is still on a

human scale. Part of the reason for this might be the recurrent decorative theme of vines and grapes, reminding visitors of man's dependence on nature. Vines feature prominently in the decoration of the pilasters, frescoes, and stucco work in the various salons. The broad upper terrace is framed by two ironwork pavilions hung with symbolic gilded suns to invite the visitor to walk in the grounds. In fact, Sanssouci is an elaborately decorated summerhouse rather than a residential palace. The palace and garden are inseparably linked, both characterized by the combination of luxury and cultural refinement. Friedrich II, the great Prussia emperor, much preferred the relative simplicity of Sanssouci to the ostentation of the New Palace, spending most of his time here. This is where he chose to die.

The flowerbeds at the foot of the terraces are more classically splendid. The perfectly straight walk and the statues scattered in the grounds are doubtless inspired by Versailles.

Queleuz

What makes Queleuz, the garden of the kings of
Portugal, so impressive is the majestic harmony
of the palace itself and the gardens it is set in, like
a jewel nestled in green velvet. It was perfectly
designed as a showcase of royal perfection. The
palace itself, like Sanssouci, has no upper floors
and seems almost modest in size. The U-shaped
building faces the principal terrace and the
garden of Neptune, a reference to the Portuguese
kings' claim to rule all the seas of the globe.
Poseidon and Athena are engaged in a struggle
that Athena will win. The collection of statues is
extremely rich and varied, featuring soldiers in
armor, grimacing monkeys, winged sphinxes
dressed up as if for a carnival, shapely nymphs,
and various mythological creatures. The most
extravagant feature of the Queleuz gardens,
however, is without doubt the canal, edged with a
stone wall lined with tiles. Today, the canal is dry,
but in centuries past, the king's guests would sail

slowly along in a procession, admiring the scenes
depicted on the tiles. These are today still as
much of a delight as ever: blue shades for
maritime scenes on the inner walls, and pink for
pastoral themes on the outer walls, both framed
in yellow. Patrick Bowe and Nicolas Sapieha

describe how the canal was once crossed by a bridge that housed a music pavilion, where an orchestra would play to the passing gondolas. Lord Kinnoul, the British envoy to the Infante Don José, told how one night, three decorated galleons, crewed by actors dressed as allegorical characters, sailed along the canal after a particularly spectacular firework display. * The gardens at Queluz also had aviaries, a menagerie, and a botanical garden, all to the glory of the king.

* Patrick Bowe and Nicolas Sapiéha, *Parcs et Jardins des plus belles demeures du Portugal* (Paris, Menges, 1990).

Schönbrunn

Schönbrunn
Johann Fischer von Erlach,
1714–1778,
Vienna, Austria

The Schönbrunn gloriette in fact stands where the palace was planned: it proved cheaper to build the palace at the bottom of the hill. The perspective over the flowerbeds and the great fountain, and up the slope to this monumental folly is all the more stunning for it. In a corner of the park is an imitation ancient ruin, a testimony to the eighteenth-century taste for the classical past.

For their summer residence, the Habsburgs chose a delightful spot—a corner of woodland on a hill close to the centre of Vienna. Their wish was to build a palace and gardens that would be even more impressive and elaborate than the Hofburg palace in the city center.

Visitors usually arrive in Schönbrunn from the city centre. The first thing to meet their eyes is the collection of buildings all painted the famous Habsburg yellow, with brown roofs. The palace itself is vast, but very harmoniously designed. The most striking sight, however, is the gloriette, which almost overshadows the rest of the park, so magnificent are the arcades round the triumphal arch, on which the imperial eagle stands proud. The vastness of this folly is even more impressive when seen doubled in its reflection in the smooth waters of a pond, placed to mirror it exactly. At the foot of the hill, Neptune's fountain, equally vast, is framed by two gently sloping ramps that lead down to the palace. The grounds also house several other features typical of this style of garden, such as a Roman ruin as a reminder of the family's ancient roots, a menagerie like those favored by medieval kings, and a greenhouse to signify imperial domination over the laws of nature.

Caserte

Caserte
Luigi Vanvitelli, 1752–1773,
Caserte, Italy

There are two standard views of
Caserte: the vast cascade
pounding down to the groups
of statues that grace the bottom
of the hill, and the more
intimate English garden
hidden under the trees,
where the water flows calmly,
tired by its mad race.

The taste for ostentatious displays of power
scales new heights in Caserte. The Bourbons of
Naples did not know the meaning of the word
humility. Several dozen miles north of Naples,
they built a palace and gardens to rival
Versailles—the queen was none other than
Marie-Antoinette's sister. The king of Naples
wanted his palace to be even more magnificent
than the palace of La Granja, built by his
father, the king of Spain.

The broad avenue and cascade lead downhill
for a distance of nearly just under two miles
(three kilometers). Halfway down is a pond
dedicated to Diana the huntress, represented in
various sculptures: attempting to dissuade
Adonis from going hunting or setting her dogs
on Acteon who had the misfortune to glimpse
her bathing nude. The Bourbons did not do
things by halves: the park is so big (and the climb
back up the hill so steep) that it is tempting to
hop into one of the little coaches or buses that
take visitors around Caserte. The lavishness of
the palace and gardens is so outrageous as to be
almost laughable, although no doubt these back-
water aristocrats, forever in the shadow of their

more sophisticated relatives, saw the expense as a way of asserting their own importance. In the late eighteenth century, Lord Hamilton ordered a second garden to be laid out, hidden in the right-hand part of the park. It is a charming corner, full of winding paths, gently flowing cascades, carefully selected trees, and elegant sculptures—the absolute antithesis of the vainglorious principal garden, which was as decadent as the family that owned it.

The Villa Giusti and other extravaganzas

The main walk through the gardens of the Villa Giusti, in the heart of Verona, leads straight up to a cliff face topped with a huge cannon. At the foot of the cliff, low hedges divide the space into various zones, creating a noble melancholy atmosphere. Nowadays the gardens are overshadowed by venerable old trees. The Giusti family was self-assured enough not to need ostentatious displays of power. They knew what they represented, and even more importantly, they knew that their rivals also knew it. The same holds true of the Pitti family, who commissioned the Boboli gardens in Florence. They devoted their energies to building up a superb collection of sculptures and creating esoteric garden styles and plant collections. To underline their scorn of attention-seeking displays of wealth and power,

they grouped together their finest treasures in the famous Boboli grotto, which was full of magnificent sculptures, frescoes, and stucco work.

The Villa Buonaccorsi, near Ancona, shows off an outstanding collection of baroque sculptures. The pride of the princes de Ligne at Beloeil, in Belgium, was the magnificent display of hornbeam hedges which today stand over thirteen feet (four meters) tall and measure several miles in length. The job of trimming the hedge several times a year is a full-time occupation.

The gardens of the châteaux of Sceaux and Meudon near Paris, both designed by Le Nôtre, symbolise power in their broad perspectives that dominate the surrounding landscape. The same is true of palaces all over Europe, from Brühl in Germany to Blenheim in England and the Royal Palace in Madrid.

The Parc André-Citroën
Gilles Clément, 1984—1993, Paris, France
The Parc de Bercy
Bernard Huet, 1994, Paris, France
The Jardin des Tuileries
André Le Nôtre, 1664, Paris, France

In the Parc de Bercy (above), the walks and banks of flowers were planned round the former wine warehouses. The Parc André-Citröen (right and facing page) was built on an industrial wasteland. The designer thus had carte blanche to come up with an extremely innovative scheme including some stunning greenhouses. In the Tuileries (following double spread), the idea was to retain as much as possible of Le Nôtre's original layout. Exuberant flowerbeds bring a flourish of modernity to the rather staid gardens.

The Parc André-Citroën and the Banks of the Seine

The banks of the Seine, running through the heart of Paris, are lined with gardens which are a vital part of the panorama of city life. They line up along the river like flotilla of ships. Gardens have always been part of the Paris cityscape, from the Jardin des Plantes in the east of the city to Invalides, the Champ de Mars, Trocadéro, and very modern gardens such as the Parc André-Citroën Cévennes in the west or the Parc de Bercy in the east. Over the centuries, the city authorities have considered it a source of prestige to have a series of gardens strung along the river like a rope of pearls round the neck of a Parisian beauty.

Gardens of Knowledge

From the collections of rare trees in ancient Abyssinia to the gardens of Hatshepsut, Queen of Egypt, from the philosophical walks of the Greeks and the groves of statues of the Romans to the collections of medicinal plants in medieval monasteries, gardens have always attracted the finest scientific and cultural thinkers of every civilization. Gardens can be seen as the crystallization of the scientific thought of the day: details such as the layout of the walks and the choice of landscape reflect contemporary trends in geometry, physics, and even philosophy. Plants brought back from distant voyages of exploration, variations on a given architectural theme, technical innovations in terms of irrigation or protection from inclement weather—every facet of a garden bears the stamp of its time.

The Pleasure Pavilion in Laeken, an engraving in *Choix des Monuments, édifices et maisons les plus remarquables du Royaume des Pays-Bas* by Pierre Jacques Goetghebuer, 1827. Private collection.

The Eden Project

Tim Smit, 1990, Saint Austell, Cornwall, England

Enormous transparent domes protect the fragile, exotic jungle flora from the rigours of the British climate, while teaching visitors about various ecosystems.

In 1990 Tim Smit, a music producer, was traveling around Cornwall when he came across an abandoned eighteenth-century garden called Heligan. He fell in love immediately, and decided to devote himself to bringing the site back to life, despite having no prior knowledge of gardening. The seeds were sown for one of the great late twentieth century gardening adventures, when a few years later, Tim Smit began looking around for a site for his next project. He finally found the perfect spot some fifteen miles away in an abandoned china clay pit near the sea, not far from the town of Saint Austell. Tim Smit's plan for what came to be known as the Eden Project was to create a series of biospheres protected from the inclement British weather by geodesic domes made of light steel struts and sheets of transparent plastic covering most of the quarry. Each is 656 feet broad by 328 feet long, and stand 187 feet tall (200 meters broad by 100 meters long, and stand 57 meters tall). The biotopes include a humid South American forest, tropical islands with an oceanic climate, and the Cameroon jungle. Visitors are whisked from Malaysia to the Mediterranean coast, from California to South Africa. One of the star attractions is a waterfall that pounds down over ninety-eight feet (thirty meters).

In the tropical greenhouse, visitors are subjected to temperatures of 95 °F (35 °C) degrees in the shade. They walk through a forest of bamboos, mahogany trees, and vanilla plants. The industrial applications of various plants are also highlighted: hevea is used in tyres, and anatto is used in hair dye, for example. An exhibition focuses on certain plants that have had a major impact on our Western lifestyle, giving us such familiar goods as chocolate or chewing gum. The credo behind the Eden Project is that mankind has caused great devastation in many parts of the world, but that there are still some pristine areas where man and nature live in harmony. Visitors to the site learn about the marvels of the plant kingdom and made to realize that they too have a role to play in saving the planet.

The Eden Project has been a huge popular success. Its ambitions reach far beyond those of traditional greenhouses: it actually proposes a new vision of man's relationship with the world we live in. Other greenhouse developments have since followed suit. The new botanical garden in Bordeaux, although on a much smaller scale, draws on the same philosophy to teach visitors about the ecology of south-western France.

Portrack

Charles Jencks and Maggie Keswick, 1990, Portrack, Dumfriesshire, Scotland

The astonishing Portrack garden, created in 1990, is based on a design inspired by chaos theory. Similarly, in the eighteenth century, Newton's discoveries in the world of physics led people to think about space in a completely new way.

The gardens of Portrack House, Dumfriesshire, is inspired by the latest scientific thinking. The architects Charles Jencks and Maggie Keswick worked on a highly original experiment in this corner of Scotland for some years. The principle they based their work on was drawn from treatises on Chinese geomancy and their extensive knowledge of chaos theory. Charles Jencks believes that the universe is more creative, predetermined, and unpredictable than was generally acknowledged twenty years ago. He was inspired by new scientific thinking to design the curving gardens at Portrack. The influence of the Chinese style of garden is also apparent in the curves expressing the vital energy that is the essence of the site. The curves determine the exact placing of the ponds, the slope of the hill, and the open expanse of the horizon. A terrace displays a symmetrical barrier of rounded stone walls that seem to tangle together. The garden's main perspective is dominated by the specially raised hill that thrusts upwards in a spiral, in an obvious reference to the Tower of Babel. This unique garden is entirely based on the most up-to-date scientific knowledge, and thus follows in the tradition of the great eighteenth-century landscape architects, who also drew on the technological innovations of their day.

Gardens of learning

For this section, we have decided to bend the rules a little, and begin with two contemporary gardens, simply because today's designs—Méry-sur-Oise, Portrack, the Eden Project—are easily as intellectually stimulating as any of the great gardens of the past when it comes to looking at the part science has to play in the world of gardens.

Science first entered the garden as soon as men tried to keep weeds down or encourage pollination by keeping bees. Gardens have always been used to showcase the latest agricultural techniques or precious botanical collections. In the Middle Ages, each monastery had a patch of land given over to growing medicinal plants, or simples, as they were called. After the Renaissance, it was universities like Coimbra in Portugal, Padua in Italy, or Montpellier in France that had the richest plant collections, for the benefit of the medical students. This tradition has continued to the present day: plants are still at the cutting edge of medical research. Even the most familiar plants of the European countryside can have much to teach us in terms of traditional herbal remedies. Aspirin, for example, was originally extracted from willow bark, and Saint John's wort is being pioneered as a treatment for depression.

Administrators and missionaries in the far-flung British, Spanish, Portuguese, and Belgian colonies collected specimens, which were often kept in quarantine in botanical gardens in the colonies, such as Pamplemousses, or on an isolated mountainside, like Orotrava, for a while, before being sent back home. These exotic species were sometimes treated with a certain degree of suspicion. Thus in Buçaco, they were isolated in a walled garden where they presented no risk to the indigenous plant species. Elsewhere they were displayed with pride as evidence of the nation's great place on the world stage, in the Estufa Fria in Lisbon or in Kew, near London. In the closing years of the nineteenth century, collections belonging to wealthy amateurs began to rival the major royal and national collections. One of the finest botanical gardens in Europe was founded by a tea merchant at the home that bears his name—the Villa Hanbury. More recently, one of the greatest gardens of the late twentieth century, the Eden Project, was created thanks to the unceasing efforts of one man with a passion for ecology and a burning desire to pass his message on to future generations.

In the twentieth century, garden design became more democratic. It was no longer

the preserve of royalty, the nobility, and the extremely wealthy. Some of the most interesting gardens are those planned with the most modest means, such as Derek Jarman's garden or Charles Jencks and Maggie Keswick's design at Portrack, which was inspired by a new scientific development—chaos theory. Some were more artistically inclined, such as the modernist masterpiece of Roberto Burle-Marx or Walter de Maria's Lightning Field—which is in itself a fantastic lesson in elementary climatology. Others were commissioned by local or city authorities with their educational value in mind, incorporating nature trails, butterfly houses, menageries, and other attractions to get visitors thinking about their natural surroundings.

Gardens are a fabulous way of getting people, children in particular, interested in the environment. Many city authorities have realized the value of their parks and gardens as a learning resource, and are building up specialized collections of anything from baobabs to begonias to introduce their visitors to the splendors of the natural world.

The Rayol garden, near Le Lavandou on the French Riviera, was acquired by the French coastline agency in 1989. Since then, Gilles Clément has recreated the original botanical collections, including trees that can withstand Australian bush fires—a vital skill in this part of the world, regularly ravaged by summer fires. The garden's managers hope to teach visitors about the infinitely precious and fragile coastal ecosystem.

The botanical garden in Padua

The botanical garden in Padua
Francesco Bonafede, 1545,
Padua, Italy

The world's first botanical
garden was founded in Padua in
1545. It has barely changed
since the sixteenth century. The
garden is based round a circular
walled garden ringed by a
stream. The plants are still
classified according to
sixteenth-century principles.

The first botanical garden in all Europe opened in
1545, in Padua, the brainchild of Francesco
Bonafede, for the nearby medical school attached
to the University of Padua. The story goes that
Bonafede chose a circular design based on the
legend of the island of Cythera in the *Dream of
Poliphilus*, a fifteenth-century Italian text. The
garden is divided into four parts, corresponding to
the sixteenth-century system of plant classifica-
tion. Each bed is bordered with stones, as was
often the case with Renaissance gardens. Many
now familiar plants were first introduced to Europe
thanks to this garden, such as the lilac (in 1565)
and potatoes (in 1590). It enjoyed the protection of
wealthy benefactors including merchants from
Venice who earned a fortune trading with distant
lands. The charm of this garden lies in its harmonious proportions, the size of the plants, and the
tranquillity of the studious atmosphere that still
reigns. It is difficult to think of another garden that
gives the visitor such a deep sense of serenity.

98 | Gardens of the world

The Holy Forest of Buçaco

The Holy Forest of Buçaco
Designer unknown, 1268–1887,
Buçaco, Portugal

The collection of trees in
Buçaco dates from the early
Renaissance. The incredible
castle was only built in the
nineteenth century. Tasmanian
ferns grow luxuriant and thick
next to Asian hydrangeas and
African and South American
coffee shrubs.

Thanks to its extremely rich heritage as a colonial power, Portugal today boasts several superb botanical gardens enriched by centuries of scientific research in far-flung corners of the globe.

Buçaco was originally an ancient and revered forest where monks would seek refuge from the temptations of the world. In 1622, women were forbidden entry to the forest, and in 1643, a papal bull was issued excommunicating anyone found harming the trees. Over 247 acres (100 hectares) of this beautiful woodland were enclosed by a wall. Over the centuries, missionaries brought back samples of plants from all over the world, such as the cedar of Goa brought back from Mexico and planted in 1653. The collections expanded rapidly in the second half of the nineteenth century. By then, the monks had been forced to leave the forest, which became the property of the state. The romantic landscape is dotted with Japanese camphor, Tasmanian ferns, black acacias from Australia, Indian myrtle, olive trees, and Douglas firs. An extravagant castle in the style popularized by King Manuel the Great gives the garden a finishing flourish of romance. It was built for the king, but he never lived there. It has now been transformed into a luxury hotel.

Coimbra and the Estufa Fria in Lisbon

The botanical garden in Coimbra is still very much a part of the ancient and prestigious university. The plants are a serious object of study, in particular for the medical students. The garden was founded in the eighteenth century by the Marquis de Pombal in a typically French style, with terraces and symmetrical walks. In the early nineteenth century, the collections already held more than four thousand plants, and were growing steadily, in particular thanks to a program of plant exchanges with Australia which brought some forty species of eucalyptus to Europe, along with acacias that have since run wild in the north of the country, destroying much of the local flora.

The most unusual of Portugal's botanical gardens is, without doubt, the Estufa Fria (cold greenhouse) in Lisbon. It is a variation on the theme of a greenhouse, made of wooden boards designed to protect and at the same time highlight the collection of rare plants. The climate in the Portuguese capital is sufficiently clement to make traditional greenhouses made of glass

panes unnecessary. Rather, the gardeners need to shade the plants from the sun. The building is an impressive sight, as is the setting itself, on the rock face of an abandoned quarry. The wooden boards are held up by cast iron columns. Dating from the early twentieth century, the design reflects the modernist and technical preoccupations of its day. Originally, it was not planned to open the site, dedicated to Edward VII, king of England, to the public, as its primary duty was to protect the rare and precious samples of plants brought back from the Portuguese colonies. However, the mock rocaille features, grottoes, and ponds, and the delightful atmosphere soon had the people of Lisbon clamoring for visits.

The site of Estufa Fria has grown over the years, and now covers nearly two and a half acres (one hectare). To begin with, the site was mainly for shade-loving plants such as ferns, busy lizzies, strelitzia, orchids, and so on. More recent extensions to the buildings have varied the amount of light, so that now rare trees like the South American Bela sombra can be seen.

Pamplemousses
Designer unknown, 1735,
Pamplemousses, Mauritius

The calm ponds of the
Pamplemousses botanical
garden are home to a fine
collection of water-lilies,
including the world's largest,
the species *Victoria regia* (right).

Pamplemousses

The first botanical garden devoted to the plants of the tropics was founded in 1735 in Pamplemousses, in Mauritius. There was a technical and economic rationale behind the new garden: to bring together in one site all the botanical discoveries made by the colonial administrators, and to collate and examine them before transporting them in the best possible conditions back to France. Dozens of other gardens were created for the same reasons all over the world. Plants discovered in the far-flung corners of the Spanish empire were taken to the Orotrava gardens in Tenerife before they were allowed onto the Spanish mainland. To this day, in the few remaining truly wild corners of the island, you can occasionally find rare plants or trees forgotten by some long-dead colonial importer, that have flourished in a state of healthy neglect over the centuries.

Pamplemousses itself grows many decorative plants and flowers that are now widespread thanks to florists and garden centers, but that a century—or even fifty years—ago were still wildly exotic. The lotuses are nearly as admired as the giant leaves of the *Victoria regia* water lily. The palm collection, justly famous, has seeded

many other collections in botanical gardens throughout Europe. The credo of botanical gardens has always been to encourage the exchange of knowledge to further our acquaintance with the natural world. Other well-known tropical botanical collections include gardens in Singapore and the fabulously rich Bogor, in Java, which the Dutch colonisers called Buitzenborg, or "free of cares"—Sanssouci by another name.

Kew

Decimus Burton and
Richard Turner, 1844–1848,
London, England

The elegant glass and iron
frame of the Palm House in
Kew was built in the mid-
nineteenth century. It houses
an impressive collection of
palm trees and climbing plants.

Kew

The British have always enjoyed a reputation as exceptional gardeners, and Kew Gardens in the outskirts of London is one of the finest. Kew is one of the best botanical gardens to be found anywhere in the world. Founded in 1772, the gardens cover 120 hectares and are home to thousands of plant species from all over the world. Since the British Empire reached into all corners of the globe, the collection is uniquely rich, and the site today also houses a major botanical research center. The grounds are spacious, with broad green lawns alternating with display beds and magnificent, venerable old trees. Part of the park reflects the eighteenth-century mania for landscaping, such as the famous pagoda or the folly representing a ruin of a Roman arch created by William Chambers in 1761. However, the real highlight of a visit to Kew is the collection of greenhouses. Between 1844 and 1848, Richard Turner and Decimus Burton worked on a superb palm house. The tradition was brought up to date in the late 1980s with the construction of a new series of greenhouses built using the most modern techniques.

From Laeken to Saint-Jean-Cap-Ferrat

Laeken
Alphonse Balat, 1876,
Laeken, Belgium

Villa Les Cèdres
Harold Peto, 1900,
Saint-Jean-Cap-Ferrat, France

King Leopold of Belgium was a keen amateur botanist, and built some of the largest greenhouses in Europe in Laeken (facing page) to protect the rare and fragile species brought back from the colonies. He replanted sun-loving species at the Villa les Cèdres (above), which still has one of the finest plant collections on the French Riviera.

On the outskirts of Brussels stands the palace of Laeken, set in magnificent grounds. The greenhouses make Laeken a truly special place. In the past, the Belgian colonial empire meant they could collect specimens from far-flung corners of the globe. The principal greenhouse, topped with a rotunda, was built in 1876 by Alphonse Balat. Over the years, more and more shelters were built to shield the fragile plants from the sometimes harsh Belgian weather. In the early twentieth century, King Albert, a very keen amateur botanist, decided to create an exceptional collection of exotic plants in a more forgiving climate. He chose the Villa Les Cèdres in Saint-Jean-Cap-Ferrat on the French Riviera as the perfect site.

An impressive gateway leads into the grounds of the Cap Ferrat gardens. The park which King Albert I of Belgium commissioned today belongs to the Marnier-Lapostolle family. While the gardens of the Villa les Cèdres are still a well-kept secret, with relatively few visitors, the gardeners who look after the collections are truly passionate about their work. They only wish there were more of them to lavish their attention on the garden's treasures, including thirty varieties of bamboo, carnivorous plants out in the open, and dozens of species of palms, citrus fruit trees, and cacti. Altogether, there are some twenty greenhouses devoted to the botanical collections covering twelve thousand species. Among the specimens are the only variety of jasmine native to Europe, giant Echiums, sago palms, and Tillandsias, which are unusual plants that look like the grey beards of old men, and prefer to grow on trees rather than in the earth.

The Villa Hanbury

The Villa Hanbury
Ludovico Winter, 1867,
Menton, France

The Villa Hanbury, on the
French-Italian border, is second
perhaps only to the Villa les
Cèdres in terms of its botanical
collections. The exceptionally
sunny climate means the
garden can grow such exotic
species as araucarias,
Macadamia nuts, *Samuela
carnesorana*, or the scarlet
blooms of *Brunsvigia josephinae*.

Arriving at la Mortola, also known as the Villa
Hanbury, I am immediately struck by the
extraordinary magnificence of the site—a bluff
overlooking the Mediterranean on the border
between France and Italy. Here, in the 1860s, the
Hanbury brothers put together a botanical garden
of exceptional quality. By 1912, the garden had
5,800 different species. The best way to visit it is to
stroll down towards the ocean through the collection of succulents and aloes and past the magnificent trees. Soon, we arrive at the Dragon fountain,
a bronze basin guarded by a furious-looking,
water-spouting dragon, acquired in Kyoto. One of
the Villa Hanbury's boasts is the most northerly
papyrus plants of any Mediterranean garden.

Another is the pagoda with the elegantly curved
walls. Each pillar provides support for at least
three different climbing plants, and these days
they bear a fine collection of trumpet creepers.
Perhaps the most charming feature is the small
pink pavilion that stands below the villa. Back in
the main garden again we pass the Moorish
mausoleum where the Hanbury brothers are
buried, and continue on down towards the waters
of the Mediterranean, through the citrus orchards
and an olive grove with trees several centuries old.
The path leads through a pine plantation before
the garden gives way to the beach and an old
shepherd's path traced by generations of locals
who roamed the hills with their flocks long before
the villa was thought of.

The Villa Carlotta

The Villa Carlotta
Giorgio Clerici, 1745,
Tremezzo, Italy

The Villa Carlotta, facing
Tremezzo, looks demurely
classical at first glance, but
is home to richly eclectic
collections of rhododendrons
and bamboo. A stream flows
through the garden, watering
the moss, papyrus, and arum
lilies in the ponds.

The Villa Carlotta stands in seventeen acres
(seven hectares) of parkland, facing east, in
Tremezzo on the shores of Lake Como. The villa
itself dates from the eighteenth century, but
owes its fame as a tourist destination to its
gardens. In April and May, the grounds are a riot
of color thanks to the 150 rhododendrons and
azaleas that carpet the park. The botanical collections here are likewise outstanding, including
cedars, cypresses, auracarias, tulip trees,
camphor trees, eucalyptus, myrtles, grenadines,
jasmine, orange, lemon, and grapefruit trees,
and bergamot, a collection of bromeliaceas and
another of orchids. In total, there are over five
hundred varieties, not counting annuals or
bulbs. There is a graceful little Japanese
bamboo garden and, in a shady valley overhung
with tall trees, a collection of ferns. The garden
descends the slope in a series of terraces,
revealing a pergola of lemon trees which remain
outside all year round, thanks to the exceptionally mild climate. Cheeky garden gnomes peek
from the corners of the fountain, and a double
staircase overgrown with roses leads up to the
villa. There is a magnificent view round every
corner, of the villa itself, of shady copses, the
blue mountains on the horizon, or the skyline
of the nearby town of Bellaggio. It is truly a
stunning sight.

Roberto Burle-Marx's garden

Roberto Burle-Marx began his artistic career in the 1930s. He was a painter and sculptor, but first and foremost a landscape architect. He considered the gardens he designed to be works of art in their own right. His paintings and sculptures were inspired by the Modernist movement and is similar in many ways to the art of Picasso, Arp, Calder, and Léger. His garden creations were in the same tradition as those designed for the wealthy aristocrat Charles de Noailles by Paul and André Vera in Paris and Marcel Guevrekian in Grasse, on the French Riviera. He used flowerbeds to place swathes of color in the strict geometric design of the garden as a whole. This focus on garden art led to the cancellation of a planned retrospective of his oeuvre in one of the gardens at the Centre Pompidou in Paris in the late 1980s, since the authorities of the national museum of modern art in Paris decided that his paintings and sculpture were not significant enough on their own to warrant a major exhibition.

Roberto Burle-Marx began work on his garden laboratory on a former coffee plantation in San Antonio de Bica in 1949. There, he brought together the thousands of plants he had gathered on his travels to create a unique garden that seems to have been carved straight out of the jungle and is permanently on the brink of returning to its original wild state. The garden was a thrilling place to visit while Roberto Burle-Marx was still alive, as he never rested on his laurels and was always improvising challenging new displays. Always thirsty for knowledge, he saw his garden as a unique tool that would help him in his search for new heights of artistic achievements. To a lesser extent, the same can be said of Jacques Wirtz's garden in Schoten, near Antwerp.

Roberto Burle-Marx's garden
1949, San Antonio de Bica, Brazil

Roberto Burle-Marx worked on improving and his experimental garden to the very end of his life.

The Chinese garden, Montreal

Created in 1990 as part of the Montreal botanical gardens, this is the largest Chinese-style garden outside of China. It was laid out in a mere six months by a team of fifty gardeners who spoke only Chinese, and were thus left to get on with the job entirely on their own—they even grew their own vegetables on the site!

After six months, they had created the ideal Chinese garden, a place of contrast and yet of harmony. The layout, the design of the pavilions, the plants selected, and the rocks and water all worked together to produce the contrasting Yin and Yang that are a vital component of the centuries-old tradition of Chinese landscaping. The garden is also a haven, like in days gone by, a tranquil microcosm of nature that changes with the seasons. It is an invitation to meditate and induces men to strengthen their bond with nature. This was the credo of the project's promoters, who hoped to create a garden as like a genuine Chinese garden as possible. Visitors enter through a great stone courtyard guarded by stone lions and decorated with miniature stone landscapes that each have a particular poetic import, signifying prosperity, longevity, and so on. A moon-shaped doorway leads to a bridge that zigzags across the lake to a spit of land, on which stand the Pavilion of Friendship, the Lotus Pavilion, the Springtime Court, the Green Shadow Pavilion, and, beyond the Stone Mountain, the Tower of Condensing Clouds, and the Pavilion of Infinite Pleasantness.

The collection of plants is extremely rich, including over five hundred trees and thousands of evergreen plant species. The plants on display have all been chosen for their symbolic significance over thousands of years of Chinese history. This means that the rarest plants are not represented, as their very scarcity means they do not have a specific role to play in Chinese folklore. Although the harsh Canadian climate means the choice of plants is somewhat restricted, visiting the garden is nonetheless a delightful and exotic experience, and the illusion is perfect. It is hard to believe that we are in North America rather than the mysterious Far East.

Recreational Gardens

A garden is an ideal world in miniature, an attempt to recreate a perfect setting. Children love nothing better than being let loose to run wild in a garden, playing hide and seek behind the bushes. They splash in the shallows of a pond which becomes a dangerous, shark-infested ocean and climb trees to perch in tree-houses that are mighty jungle fortresses. Adults, too, enjoy playing in gardens, and over the centuries have devised countless games and amusements, from erotic statues hidden in isolated copses to elaborate box hedge mazes and treasure trails.

In the eighteenth century, the garden was often a metaphor
for discovering the secrets of life, both philosophical and erotic.
Jean-Antoine Watteau, *The Pilgrimage to Cythera*, 1717,
Musée du Louvre, Paris, France.

The Tarot Garden, Garavicchio

Niki de Saint-Phalle, 1980-1995, Capalbio, Tuscany, Italy

Inspired by Antonio Gaudi's Guell park in Barcelona, Niki de Saint-Phalle's Tarot Garden includes twenty-two giant, rounded sculptures. The bright colors and countless fragments of mirror, ceramic, and glass shimmer in the sun. Below: *The Empress.*

We are in Tuscany—in Capalbio, to be precise—in the heart of a Mediterranean forest. Here and there, strange shapes peek through the treetops, in burnished gold or painted in vivid colors. From my vantage point, I can see two men who look set to start fighting, a head surrounded by sun rays, a hand studded with fragments of mirror, and a sort of disjointed scale model of a block of flats. These are just some of the garden sculptures that the artist Niki de Saint-Phalle installed here, starting in 1979. The Tarot Garden, as she named it, represents the twenty-two major arcana in a pack of tarot cards. Each is a gigantic work of art, studded with mirrors and mosaic. The game is both the sheer pleasure of the visual impact of the pieces, and spotting the surprises. Above the tower with the off-kilter windows, for example, a derisory mechanical sculpture by Jean Tinguely rotates endlessly. Lower down, a hand emerges from behind a gigantic head whose empty eyes open onto the sky. Occasionally, a visitor's head is framed in the mouth. Thousands of little mirrored squares plate the gently rounded sculptures. A kind of serpent's tail is reminiscent of the sculpted borders by Gaudi in the Guell park in Barcelona. The focal point of the Tarot Garden is the Empress. Niki de Saint-Phalle chose to set up home inside her, cooking in one breast of the figure and washing in the other.

Hellbrunn

Santino Solari, 1613, Salzburg, Austria

These stools with holes in the seats to "refresh" the guests were one of the favourite jokes of the archbishop of Salzburg Markus Sitticus. It is not known what his guests thought of them.

The best preserved historical garden devoted to recreational purposes is without doubt Hellbrunn, near Salzburg, Austria. It was the summer residence of the prince bishops of Salzburg, built in 1613 by Santino Solari on the orders of the archbishop Markus Sitticus. It has a fabulous range of water features, including arching water jets, water-powered songbirds and marionettes along the river, fountains designed to spray the unwary visitor, a hydraulic organ, and even a table surrounded by stools, each of which had a hole in the seat to refresh the posterior of the guests! In all, there are some thirty water games. The fashion for water games came from Italy, and examples survive in many gardens throughout Italy and Germany. Many of the water features still catch out the unwary stroller, particularly at the Villa Caprile, near Pesaro, or the Villa Torregiani, near Lucca. The Wind Grotto at the latter was notorious for spraying visitors, and apparently on the hottest days of summer it was very popular with scantily clad young nymphs…

Variations on a theme

Niki de Saint-Phalle's sculpture garden in Garavicchio, Italy, created in the last years of the twentieth century, is based on the theme of a set of tarot cards. Five hundred years ago, a similarly playful theme might have been a dream journey, and in the eighteenth century, a journey to the mythical island of Cythera, home to the goddess Venus. Gardens have traditionally been associated with liberty and adventure, whether in love or in play—and after all, love is the most serious of games. Gardens are dedicated to pleasure, and so it is only natural that they should include games— a croquet lawn, a copse perfect for playing hide-and-seek, a maze—and even occasionally tricks to catch out the unwary visitor. The archbishop of Salzburg delighted in inviting his guests to sit on the chairs with a water spout in the seat in the grounds of his palace in Hellbrunn. The tradition of pleasure gardens is centuries old. In the Roman empire, gardens often witnessed scenes of decadence—the famous murals in Pompeii give an idea of the kind of licentious behaviour that went on in Roman gardens! The Middle Ages and the Renaissance were more chaste. At most, a lovelorn poet would compare the pale cheeks and cherry lips of his beloved to a rose. By the eighteenth century, times had changed again. Gardens became more private, less ostentatious, and thus once more lovers were able to while away the hours in shady corners, away from prying eyes. One hundred years later, the garden had become a bourgeois status symbol, and followed the moral and aesthetic precepts of the society of the day.

Twentieth-century gardens have tended to search further afield for their influences than was hitherto the case: Maulévrier and Biddulph Grange both draw on an Oriental style, for instance. Another style that has been in and out of fashion over the decades is mosaiculture, the proper name for floral displays in the shape of a given object, where

the plants are used not so much for themselves as for their colour and texture. The origins of mosaiculture can be traced back to the fifteenth century, when it was fashionable to grow low box hedges that spelt out philosophical maxims. Many garden historians see the next stage in the development of this unusual art form in the decorative flowerbeds of the sixteenth and seventeenth centuries. In the nineteenth century, floral displays, for example of ducks or train locomotives, became increasingly popular. In the same vein, the Italian region of Pistoia was renowned in the sixteenth century for its topiary caricatures.

Gardeners would fashion metal frames in the desired shape—a portrait of the prince or the latest addition to his private zoo—and trim their privets to the required shape.

The signs are that the twenty-first century will perhaps not be as inventive as centuries gone by. Today, gardens play at being exotic in theme parks, where nature is little more than a stage setting—a jungle, a desert, a savannah, a forest. We can but hope that landscape architects will break free of this rather utilitarian vision of gardens as a backdrop to other attractions, and that once again, gardening will be recognized as an art form in its own right.

The grounds of Groussay (Monfort-l'Amaury, France) are dotted with architectural follies in the Palladian style beloved of Emilio Terry.

The Villa Reale

The Villa Reale
Designer unknown,
seventeenth century, Marlia, Italy

The great fishpond in Marlia (right) is some way distant from the villa. The statues represent the great rivers of Italy, just as certain statues in Versailles represent the rivers of France.

Not far from Garavicchio, a cubic house stands in splendid isolation in the middle of a borad esplanade of lawn and gravel walks. It does not look a very inviting place to live. The garden, however, is one of the loveliest in all Tuscany. It has had the good fortune to be in the hands of passionate gardeners over the last three centuries, all of whom have contributed to the multi-faceted splendor of the grounds today. First of all there is the great park in the English style, with magnificent views and copses of rare trees. After admiring the villa, which from a distance looks as if it is moored in a sea of lawns, we come to a pleasantly welcoming part of the grounds. In hot weather, the water features in the Renaissance pavilion splash passers-by with refreshing spray. Nearby is a delightful old villa surrounded by box hedges and banks of flowers. The walk takes us on through the undergrowth along the channels that in years gone by gushed full of water. We pass several eighteenth-century fishponds, water jets, and fountains. We are in the heart of the eighteenth-century open-air garden theater, with white statues dotted around under

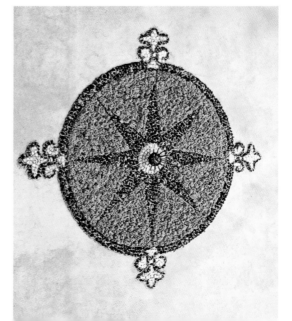

the yew trees. Each represents a character from the Commedia dell'Arte—Harlequin, Colombine, or Pulcinella. Retracing our steps, we come across a most unexpected sight. Behind a wall is a superb Art Deco garden in an imitation of the Arabic style, studded with colored earthenware tiles, designed in the 1920s by the French landscape architect Jacques Greber. We carry on between two avenues lined with tall topiaried trees, round to the back of the villa, where we discover the huge fountain with its mossy cascades. We spend a pleasant half-hour exploring the fountain, slipping on the edges of the pools and splashing each other childishly. The gardens of the Villa Reale are the perfect example of an aristocrat's hideaway, designed exclusively for pleasure.

Villandry
Joachim Carvallo, 1906,
Villandry, France

The gardens at Villandry were
laid out in the early twentieth
century to a plan inspired by
the Renaissance. Above: The
vegetable garden, planted by
color. Facing page: The low box
hedges and flowerbeds of the
ornamental garden were
inspired by embroidery
patterns.

Villandry

When Joachim Carvallo set out to create the
gardens at Villandry, he may not have had
games in mind. However, as early as 1906, he
began to enjoy playing with the notion of variations on a theme. His creation drew inspiration
from Pacello di Mercogliano, the gardening
monk, who designed the Renaissance gardens
in Blois, Gaillon, and Bury. Carvallo based
every aspect of his design on reliable historical
sources, from the beds of the ornamental
garden and the symbolism of their flowers to
the plantations in the vegetable patch, the
maze, and the bowers. Arab-Andalusian
elements are placed side by side with flowered
meadows, and Art Nouveau benches stand
next to topiary designs that would not look
out of place in Versailles. In the great tradition
of landscape art, this happy-go-lucky mix of
elements bears witness to the richness of each
century's contribution to the art of gardening.
The result is a joyous confusion of styles that
leaves visitors bewildered, but exhilarated.

Biddulph Grange and Maulévrier

Biddulph Grange and Maulévrier are two fine examples of the Oriental style of garden. Visitors to Biddulph Grange in England are greeted by four sphinxes and an Egyptian temple. A series of wooden bridges takes them to the Chinese garden, along a walk that betrays an eclectic mixture of exotic Far Eastern influences—Chinese, Japanese, and Khmer, with touches of Egypt thrown in.

Alexandre Marcel, the architect who designed the garden at Maulévrier for his father-in-law, created an Oriental atmosphere by acquiring second-hand material from the 1900 Universal Exhibition held in Paris, including a Khmer temple, serpents' heads, lanterns, and Buddhas. He set them round a small lake, and planted a number of Far Eastern species of trees to protect them. The illusion of a classical seventeenth-century Japanese garden is perfect.

Biddulph Grange
James Bateman and Edward Cooke, 1850, Biddulph, England

The Oriental park, Maulévrier
Alexandre Marcel, 1894–1917, Maulévrier, France

Above: The sphinxes at Biddulph Grange watch over the grounds, which have echoes of Egyptian and Japanese garden design.
Left: The harmonious garden in Maulévrier reflects the influence of various Eastern philosophies.

The Villa Ile de France:
a patchwork of styles

The Villa Ile de France in Saint-Jean-Cap-Ferrat and Vizcaya in Florida may be separated by thousands of miles, but they have one thing in common: both play with eclectic architectural references in the same way.

The villa in the elegant resort of Cap-Ferrat on the French Riviera is an astonishing, almost comical sight. It resembles a monstrous pink wedding cake, the windows framed in white stone so many puffs of whipped cream. It is quite a challenge to recognize the architectural references—here a Venetian window, there an Arabic one, a double door, Spanish stucco work, a classical salon, and a touch of Old England. A little further on, in the garden, is a classical canal directly in line with the villa. It is edged with a triple flower border crossed by Japanese stepping stones. Behind there is a romantic rockery that leads up to a temple devoted to Love. Along the walk are scattered Italian pottery, carved stone urns and fruit baskets, and cement seats shaped like tree trunks.

Lower down is a Spanish garden filled with pergolas, narrow channels, and a profusion of climbing plants. Then we come to the stone garden, a fascinating collection of archaeological relics—there was not enough room in the villa itself for everything the Baroness Ephrussi de Rothschild acquired in her travels round Europe—and a Japanese garden. On the far side is a Provençal garden, which needs a lot of work to keep it looking so charmingly unkempt! The garden of the Villa Ile de France is not only a delightful place for a stroll, it is also a fabulous history lesson on the eclectic tastes of the Belle Epoque.

Another equally intriguing, through more recent, garden, dating from the second quarter of the twentieth century, is to be found in Vizcaya. This Italianate villa, built in 1916, was the winter residence of a wealthy industrialist. The references here are Isola Bella, the famous garden on Lake Maggiore, and the Barcaccia fountain in Rome, sculpted by Bernini. The villa is most ornate, with square towers on each corner and a roof of curved tiles, a profusion of peristyles and windows inspired by the Renaissance architecture of Sebastiano Serlio. The grounds are just as decorative, with bands of flowerbeds that resemble strips of embroidered cloth, ornamental ponds and cascades, small villas by the water, and an elegantly rounded Chinese bridge, in a setting of luxuriant greenery.

The Amusing Topiary Garden : floral displays

The Amusing Topiary Garden
Anonymous, 2001,
Chaumont-sur-Loire, France

Tracce
Roberto Capecci, Marco Antonini,
and Raffaele Sini, 2001, Villa Oliva,
Lucca, Italy

Above: the Amusing Topiary Garden in Chaumont-sur-Loire creates an atmosphere worthy of the paintings of Henri Rousseau. Right: These innovative waves of greenery show that topiary is casting off its stilted classical image and coming into the twenty-first century.

Many gardens are based on the principle of adapting and shaping nature. An extreme example of this is the Japanese art of bonsai, in which the force of nature is bent to the will of the gardener to produce miniature trees.

The art of topiary dates back to ancient Rome. It was taken up again in the gardens of the Italian Renaissance. It consists of trimming trees or shrubs into a chosen shape, often animals or geometric forms. There is no limit to the keen gardener's imagination: the topiary elephants of King Rama of Thailand, in Bangkok, are justly famous, and stand alongside topiary turtles, cubes, spirals, airplanes, and crocodiles. The topiary designs recently recreated at Versailles give a precise idea of eighteenth-century garden fashions in France, although their British, German, and Spanish counterparts were equally imaginative. Floral displays have also come back into fashion. The displays in the shape of ducks on the island of Mainau on Lake Constance in southern Germany and the extravagantly decorated floats at the Lemon festival in Menton on the French Riviera, after years of ridicule, are now back at the cutting edge of fashion.

Theme parks: Tivoli

Tivoli
Designer unknown, nineteenth
century, Copenhagen, Denmark

Disneyland Resort Paris
Bill Morgan Evans, 1992,
Marne-la-Vallée, France

Above: Tivoli was the first of
the world's great theme parks.
The clipped, tamed view of
nature they give is very much in
evidence at Disneyland Paris
(right and facing page).

Some gardens are specifically designed as places
of recreation. This is the case of the Planten
und Blumen garden in Hamburg, or the Tivoli
Gardens in Copenhagen. There is nothing nicer
than a stroll along the walks on a sunny summer

afternoon, past a Chinese pagoda hidden round
a corner or a restaurant in a galleon moored at a
quay smothered in flowers. The Tivoli gardens,
which could be said to be the world's first
theme park, were founded in 1843. Ever since,
attractions have been added regularly, so there
is always something new to discover. It has
proved a source of inspiration for theme parks
all over the world. At the Disneyland park near
Paris, for example, great care was taken over the
gardens, which the park's designers saw as
scenery for the rides and attractions. The
Mexican zone, for example, is planted with
cacti, while the Swiss Family Robinson area is
full of plants typical of European forest habitat.
For the past few years, visitors have been able to
go on guided tours of the gardens on various
themes such as topiary and floral displays.
Mickey Mouse is proud of his gardens.

Landscaping

The moment when man first took notice of the landscape around him is lost in the mists of time. One thing is certain: our ancestors had to attain a certain degree of intellectual sophistication before they could grasp the concept of interacting with the land they lived on, by farming it, for example. Prehistoric man was first a hunter, as the numerous surviving cave paintings of animals show. Only gradually did the notion of farming a patch of land, then of gardening for pleasure, come to be accepted. In Western culture, the first paintings of largely idealized landscapes date from ancient Rome. Only in the Middle Ages did representations of landscapes become more diverse and symbolic. Paintings of enclosed gardens and manuscript illuminations of the workers in the fields reflect a desire to explore the relationship between society and the land. From the seventeenth century on, landscape painting became increasingly popular. It could symbolize the power of a feudal prince or the utopian dream of a perfect society, fear of the elements or the caress of nature in her most benevolent mood. This understanding of nature as symbolic of human society was common to Japanese borrowed scenery and Italian villas built in the heart of the countryside. The nineteenth century, the age of industrialization, brought a new vision of nature as a place of refuge from the demands of hectic city life.

A detail of the Palladian bridge at Blenheim palace. Engraving by C.V. Fielding in *Havell's History of the Thames*, 1796, Guildhall Library, London, England.

Derek Jarman's garden

Derek Jarman, 1985, Dungeness, England

This garden has been a source of hot dispute ever since it was created. Some people love it, while others cannot bear the idea of a garden of rusty old tools and weeds.

This garden is truly unique. It was planned by its owner, the film director Derek Jarman, as an impossible challenge. It is in the far south of England, by the sea, at the foot of the Dungeness nuclear power station, and lies on a bed of pebbles. Derek Jarman had been a keen amateur botanist all his life. The garden he created reflects three aspects of his personality: his artistic flair, his genuine love of plants, and his interest in the environmental movement. He put these three aspects together and came up with a magical combination of flowers, shrubs, flints, shells, and driftwood, with strange sculptures of stone, old tools, and rusty pieces of bric-a-brac dotted here and there, works of art nestling in a constantly changing setting. In autumn, the plants die and leave the stage to the circles of flints and pebble sculptures that are the focal point of the garden throughout the winter, only to disappear again with the arrival of spring, flooded by an encroaching tide of lavender and santolina.

Prospect Cottage is black with yellow window frames. It stands proud in the midst of this personal vision of paradise. In spring the cottage is surrounded by enormous purple wild cabbages. Gorse bushes grow in a circle round a stone stake. Further on, the theme is reversed: pebbles polished smooth by the North Sea have been placed in a circle round some gorse bushes. Rusty, twisted pieces of iron are half-buried under a profusion of climbing tendrils. Purplish-white wild poppies have made themselves at home. Valerian, camomile, and gillyflowers bloom all over the place, and wooden stakes tipped with iron seem to spring spontaneously from the soil. Derek Jarman explained how he planted these stakes to protect the garden like dragon's teeth, to act as stout warriors challenging anyone who protested against his unruly haven. It is without doubt the loveliest garden of weeds ever created. Derek Jarman died in 1994, without leaving his garden.

Karlsberg

Giovanni Francesco Guerniero, 1701, Kassel, Germany

The city of Kassel was built at the foot of this superb palace and its grounds. The prince truly dominated his subjects.

In Kassel, your gaze tires before it reaches the far distant horizon. Standing in the gardens of Karlsberg, in the Wilhelmshöhe park, you feel as if the lands that spread at your feet are yours for the taking. The gardens were designed to strike anyone who dared climb the hill with awe and reverence. Work began on this impressive park in 1701. A few years previously, Karl von Hessen-Kassel toured Italy, and was inspired to plan a monumental park. He commissioned

Giovanni Francesco Guerniero with the works. Guerniero designed a garden that was in fact far larger than the one actually laid out, which is impressive enough as it is. Standing on the summit of the hill, dominating the surrounding countryside, is an octagonal building topped with an obelisk. The obelisk is in turn topped with a gigantic reproduction of the statue of the Farnese Hercules (just as in Vaux-le-Vicomte). The whole structure rests on enormous foundations of huge stones piled in three levels. Three waterfalls boil down eiht hundred twenty feet (two hundred fifty meters) to a pond at the bottom of the hill dedicated to Neptune. The staircase that leads down the rocks is huge, but standing on it, you feel very small as you look down to the castle below. The impression of being an insignificant dot in the landscape is even more overwhelming when you look out towards the horizon, since you can see for many miles, right over the city and into the countryside beyond. When the castle was built,

Karl must have been able to gaze out over the whole of his lands spread at his feet. The view from the hill is the most striking expression of territorial domination and absolute power to be found anywhere in Europe. At the bottom of the waterfalls, the water pressure is so great that the spray reaches a height of one hundred sixty four feet (fifty metres). Gradually, over the decades,

the grounds were tamed and domesticated. The winding paths and pools of water artfully arranged to look as natural as possible, the follies recounting tales from Virgil or the history of China or the pyramids, meant the gardens were less obviously an expression of the prince's desire to dominate his lands. In the early nineteenth century, the mood of the garden changed again: Wilhelmsbad, a medieval ruin in the grounds, was transformed into a romantic castle decorated with the sign of the lion, the emblem of the von Hessen family. You can still gaze out over the countryside from the crenellated towers, watchtowers, and pinnacles, but the sense of absolute power has given way to a gentler vision of man's place in nature.

The eye of the beholder

These two visions of the landscape could not be more different. Facing page: the arrogance of Karlsberg, where a hill was raised so the prince could demonstrate his power. Below: Murin An is far humbler, and thus much more poetic. It seeks to frame the magic of the mythical mountain glimpsed between the trees.

Derek Jarman's aethetic vision—a garden of weeds at the foot of a nuclear power station—is certainly not to everyone's taste. But it is perfectly in phase with its time and the burning issues of the day regarding the place of the natural environment in our increasingly industrialised society. Paradoxically, the same could be said for the grandiloquent palace and grounds of Karlsberg, which could not be more different from Jarman's modest patch of land. It, too, reflects a major question of its day—the way absolutist monarchs wielded their power over their territories. There

was no room for doubt in Karlsberg. The prince intended to dominate his subjects. This desire to dominate the landscape, both physically and metaphorically, was a principal factor in the design of the great classical gardens, first in France, then in the rest of Europe.

The Suzuki archipelago is light years away from such worldly concerns. Rather, it is characterized by doubt and uncertainty, only partially soothed by the reassuringly eternal presence of the river, drifting past the shifting islands of sand.

Aesthetes have always found it a fruitful approach to concentrate on specific features of the landscape. This was very much the case in the eighteenth century, when landscape architects composed their own ideal landscapes by damming rivers and planting copses—Blenheim, Weikersheim, Schwetzingen. It was also the practice of the Japanese designers who "borrowed" natural scenery by framing it in from a particular vantage point and thus incorporating it into the narrative of the garden.

The gardener's vision of the landscape need not be very grand. Albertas, near Aix en Provence in southern France, laid out in 1751, is very modest—unusually, there is no château in the grounds. Similarly discreet are Murin An, in Kyoto, where the most showy feature is a view of a distant mountain framed between trees, and the Villa Gamberaia, nestled deep in the bosom of the Tuscan countryside.

Blenheim

England's love affair with gardens dates back hundreds of years. The heyday of British landscape design was without doubt the eighteenth century, when great names like Lancelot Brown (better known as Capability Brown) and Humphry Repton created harmonious, sweeping landscapes in keeping with the aesthetic tastes of the day. The idea was to alter the lay of the land, but so that the final result appeared natural, in contrast with the highly artificial French style.

In the grounds of Blenheim Palace, offered to the Duke of Marlborough by a grateful nation after his victory at the Battle of Blenheim, Capability Brown changed the course of the river, dug two lakes, and created an impressive

waterfall. All of the parks he worked in bear the stamp of his love of harmony: for example, trees are planted together in groves so that from a distance, they form a block of color that is balanced by another grove nearby. He preferred not to call on many of the artifices used by his fellow landscape architects, such as building a bridge to give a newly dug river a raison d'être,

or erecting a church tower peeking over the horizon as if there were a prosperous rural community in the vicinity. Capability Brown worked only with the elements that nature gave him. The author of Gothic novels Horace Walpole was a great admirer of Brown. In 1780 he wrote an essay in praise of the art of modern gardening: "We have discovered the point of perfection. We have given the true model of gardening to the world; let other countries mimic or corrupt our taste; but let it reign here on its verdant throne, original by its elegant simplicity, and proud of no other art than that of softening nature's harshnesses and copying her graceful touch."

The Palladian bridge in Blenheim (left) is typical of the eighteenth-century English style. The bridge and its reflection create a perspective that draws our gaze out into the countryside. The caryatids (above) hint at the great wealth of the Dukes of Marlborough whose family home this is.

Weikersheim

The baroque gardens in the palace of Weikersheim, Germany, are an unparalleled example of eighteenth-century German garden design. The palace itself was home to the von Hohenlohe family. It is a symmetrical building of generous proportions. The façade on the garden side is decorated with three gables. The interior is richly appointed, in particular the Hall of Knights which has a remarkable painted ceiling and unusual sculpted hunt scenes round the walls. However, the finest feature of the palace is undoubtedly the garden, which is in a delightful setting, facing a landscape of gently rolling hills. In the early eighteenth century, the architect Hans Lüttich came up with plans for an

orangery in two parts at the end of the garden. The opening between the two pavilions neatly frames a superb view, giving the impression of Japanese-style borrowed scenery. The two pavilions are in glass, which further underlines the dialogue with the surrounding landscape. There can be no doubting that the land here belongs to the von Hohenlohe family. And if there were any room for doubt as to who the masters were, the statues in the grounds clear up any remaining uncertainty. The statues along principal parterre represent the gods of Mount Olympus and the continents. The palace servants are also represented as statues, but in case being sculpted gave them ideas above their station, they were shown going about their business—as dwarves.

Schwetzingen

There are a thousand reasons to visit Schwetzingen, to marvel at the elegant layout of the gardens that form a gigantic circle intersected by an equally immense square. The design is extremely complex. The grounds are dotted with features such as the canal, a ruined folly, a mosque, a bath house, and a Chinese tea pavilion. The part I love best is a little corner of the garden. Past a latticework rotunda, where water flows from the beaks of bird sculptures, there opens a tunnel, also in latticework, that leads off to the horizon. At the far end of the tunnel, the visitor discovers a delightful country scene, with a river winding lazily by. The grass growing at the foot of the tunnel entrance give life to the scene—yet it is all an illusion. It is a brilliant trompe-l'œil painting of the landscape beyond the tunnel, and a fascinating commentary on the link between landscape and art, between reality and idealized representations of life. To my knowledge, this illusion of a painting representing a landscape in situ is unique.

Schwetzingen
Ludwig Petri, Nicolas de Pigage,
eighteenth century,
Schwetzingen, Germany

Murin An

Murin An is perhaps the finest example of the Japanese *shakkei* or "borrowed scenery" style. The garden, based round a pond, is near the heart of Kyoto, and dates back to 1896.

It is generally very narrow but broadens out in the center. It has a complex network of walks round the confluent of the two streams that flow through the gardens. The shady walks lead to a clearing with a cascade flowing down the hill. The clearing was designed to frame Kyoto's sacred mountain, Mount Hi

Hei, and the cascade is an optical illusion designed to suggest the water is flowing down the flanks of the mountain. The *shakkei* style integrates the garden into the wild scenery that forms the backdrop to the view. Murin An, like the garden of the Entsu Ji temple, both "borrow" Mount Hi Hei for its religious symbolism. As in the example of the Schwetzingen trompe-l'œil tunnel, the gardens are not designed to dominate nature but to co-exist harmoniously side by side with it.

Murin An
Ogawa Sihei, 1896, Kyoto, Japan

Murin An is a subtle contrast of light and shade, the intimacy of the sheltering trees and the inaccessible, distant landscape.

The Villa Gamberaia

The Villa Gamberaia
Johanna Ghyka, seventeenth
and nineteenth centuries,
Settignano, Italy

There are many surprises in
store at the Villa Gamberaia:
walking through the dim
arcades, then suddenly
emerging into the blinding light
of the plain, turning a corner
into a sea of olive trees, or a
stroll through the sacred wood.

Like Murin An, the Villa Gamberaia, near
Florence, in the heart of the magnificent Tuscan
countryside, reflects a deep-rooted desire for
harmony. The garden, ringed by a solid wall, looks
out over vineyards and fruit orchards. This prosperous agricultural landscape is the most charming aspect of the park. The current garden is a
recent creation, based on the original seventeenth-
century plans. An imposing yew hedge closes off
the garden, with openings selected to frame
particularly spectacular views. At the far end of the

garden, a semi-circle of arcades provides the loveliest view. As Maurice Fleurent wrote, the Villa
Gamberaia owes its power of seduction perhaps to
the harmony of lines that seem contradictory but
that in fact complement each other, and to the
juxtaposition of two perfect expressions of beauty.
This garden, on a human scale, needs to breathe,
to be part of the surrounding landscape—a landscape which naturally produced it, and with which
it forms a well-thought-out contrast. *

* Maurice Fleurent, *Le Monde Secret des Jardins*
(Paris: Flammarion, 1987).

The Parc de la Tête d'Or

Like many other cities in France, Lyon has a landscaped park that was the brainchild of the famous Bühler brothers. Between them, the two brothers created several dozen of the most significant nineteenth-century parks in France, in particular the park in Tours known as the Jardin des Prébendes d'Oé and the Parc Borely in Marseille. Their style was heavily influenced by English landscape design, and thus uses elements such as tall trees, open views, and broad, flowered lawns. The Parc de la Tête d'Or lies on the banks of the Rhône, and has a total area of over 272 acres (110 hectares). It takes a good couple of days to explore every nook and cranny: the islands scattering the lake, which covers an area of forty acres (sixteen hectares), the flowerbeds with their collections of hardy perennials, the famous rose garden with several dozen thousand roses, and the tropical greenhouses, including the great dome. Star of the aquatic plant collection is the great Victoria regia water lily, whose leaves resemble giant quiche moulds. There is also a zoo, collections of alpine plants and vines, an arboretum, and the justly celebrated wrought iron gate at the entrance to the park. What makes the park such a delightful place for a visit is that time has done its work healing the scars of the landscaping work, and the illusion is perfect: the lie of the land seems entirely natural. Strolling from one clearing to another, with pergolas nestled in the grass, there is always something new to discover. The Parc de la Tête d'Or is extremely popular with the people of Lyon who crowd the lawns as soon as the sun comes out, making it one of the best—and best-loved—public parks in Europe.

A Miniature World

Despite the differences in styles from one century and one continent to another, nearly all the gardens featured in this book share one common feature. From Hadrian's Villa to Ian Hamilton Finlay's Little Sparta, each reflects the ideal vision of nature that the owner of the garden has striven to attain—a world in miniature. Wörlitz, Stowe, and Stourhead are bucolic Arcadias. Veitshöchheim and the Petit Trianon in the grounds of Versailles are visions of a dream of absolute seclusion, far from the petty factions of aristocrats jockeying for royal favor. There is no need to seek out a Japanese Zen garden to contemplate the endless expanse of the universe. Simply lie down in the grass in your local park and watch the ants going about their business, untroubled by your vast presence.

This charmingly naive portrait of the nature philosopher Jean-Jacques Rousseau reflects eighteenth-century tastes: a peaceful river, a home nestling among the trees, and bouquets of scented blossom. Anonymous, *Jean-Jacques Rousseau in Ermenonville*, eighteenth century, Musée Carnavalet, Paris, France.

Little Sparta

Ian Hamilton Finlay, 1974, Stonypath, Scotland

Little Sparta is crowded with references to mythology and philosophy: the old farm outbuilding is now a temple to Apollo (facing page), rocks are engraved with words of the French revolutionary Saint-Just (below), and a gilded head bears the words "Apollo is a terrorist" (right).

Ian Hamilton Finlay is an unusual figure in the often rather traditional world of gardening. He is perhaps better known as a poet and sculptor. His major work is the garden he has created in Stonypath, Scotland, baptized "Little Sparta." His garden is a cultural artifact, the result of his philosophical meditations. The composition of the garden is guided by the recurrent themes of mythology and his thoughts on contemporary society. It is full of references that would not seem out of place in an eighteenth-century garden, such as the old farm outbuilding that is now a temple of Apollo, or another temple dedicated to Philemon and Baucis. The lintels above the windows of Apollo's temple bear inscriptions in praise of music, the muses—and missiles, symbols of the battles Ian Hamilton Finlay had to fight with the local authorities when he first began work on his garden. Near the lake there lie some ten stones, each carved with part of a quotation by

one of the leaders of the French Revolution, Saint-Just: "The present order is the disorder of the future." The forehead of a gilded head is engraved with the inscription "Apollo is a terrorist." Nearby, the signature of the great German artist Albrecht Dürer is carved in a stone that hangs from a tree. A stone submarine seems to be about to emerge from the waters of the lake, and the grounds are dotted with a bird table in the shape of an aircraft carrier, a miniature aqueduct, and Corinthian pillars. The overall effect is sometimes comical, but what the artist is saying about the world through his garden is utterly serious.

Hadrian's Villa

Designer unknown, 118 B.C.–38 A.D., Tivoli, Italy

The colonnade round the Canopus was built as a reference to the great power and influence of the Roman empire during the reign of Hadrian.

Ian Hamilton Finlay's artistic vision draws on a long tradition of gardens designed to create the illusion of a world in miniature. Hadrian's Villa, in Tivoli, near Rome, is a far earlier example based on the same tradition. The emperor set out to bring together symbols from all the places he had visited in his vast empire.

The villa, built on the site of the mythical city of Tibur, is set in over 296 acres (120 hectares) of parks. Although the buildings seem to have been set down haphazardly, their arrangement in fact corresponds to a series of philosophical considerations on the society of the day. The Maritime Theatre, the Canopus (an oval pool), the Academy, the thermal baths, and the Piazza d'Oro are all part of a story which was not told solely for the greater glory of the emperor, contrary to what has often been claimed. The gardens play an essential part in telling the story, since they are the link between the various edifices. The buildings play on the landscape, following the example of Pliny's villa. The park in which the buildings were set often confers a higher level of meaning to the scene as a whole.

In the Greek tradition, gardens were already sacred. They were inspired by the Persian tradition to plan their palaces in the centre of their gardens, which were designed to be earthly paradises, with streams, pools of water, grottoes, and aviaries housing exotic songbirds. Other elements were essential ingredients in creating an idyllic haven: grot-

toes, grouped statues of nymphs, circular temples to the cult of Venus, vines in homage to Dionysos, groves dedicated to the god Pan. The garden was a stage for the gods, a Mount Olympus in miniature. The woodland copses were scattered with statues of fauns, bacchantes, nymphs, Priapus, Silenus, and Venus. Nature was a pantheon.

Gardens and society

In Wörlitz, Germany, the pavilions dotted here and there in the grounds each tell a story—erotic or philosophical, depending on the visitor's point of view.

Gardens naturally reflect the society of their day—but there is also a certain timelessness, a certain universality, in the desire to create a garden out of the wilderness. For while I am transforming wasteland into a fertile, blooming garden, imitating on my own small scale the effect of the whole of mankind on the natural environment on the scale of continents, I am at the center of my own universe. Some landscape architects have been inspired to design gardens on philosophical themes. Ian Hamilton Finlay's garden, Little Sparta, has been compared to a philosophical poem in the barren Scottish heathlands. The Roman emperor Hadrian and the Chinese emperor Quian Long both had the same idea, hundreds of years and thousands of miles apart, of recreating miniature versions of the loveliest parts of their empires in their own gardens, which thus became the symbolic heart of their domains.

The garden of Wörlitz, in Germany, can be compared to what would today be termed a sociological experiment. The prince's dream was to create an ideal "garden state", where men could live harmoniously in complete autarcy. Such experiments were typical of the Age of Enlightenment, when the natural landscape was considered a mirror for human emotions. This sentiment is also apparent in the intimate groves and shady walks at Veitshöchheim and the rustic meadows of Blenheim, where sheep calmly graze almost in the shadow of the great palace.

The same philosophy was the source of the classical Japanese gardens which are conducive

to metaphysical contemplation. In Zen gardens, various stylized landscapes are offered up for meditation just a few paces apart, placing man at the heart of the natural world, represented in miniature.

These gardens often convey a sense of magical intimacy that is totally absent from crowded public parks. Only in the silence of such a garden, where the only sound is the rustling of the leaves, can one truly hear oneself think.

of the British envoy in Naples), and an imitation tomb of the nature philosopher Jean-Jacques Rousseau. The numerous bridges that criss-cross the park clearly demonstrate the prince's interest for the latest engineering innovations and techniques borrowed from civilizations all over the world. Likewise, the fruit orchards and flocks of sheep, the park all indicate his desire to demonstrate the advantages of a new society built along rational principles, where everyone and everything had an allotted place.

Many of the same principles are apparent in the gardens of Stourhead. In fact, there are gardens all over Europe that are based round similar elements, including temples to Flora or Apollo, pantheons, grottoes, Gothic mansions, metal bridges or bridges designed in the Palladian style, and cascades.

The gardens at Stowe include a version of the Elysian Fields, a Temple of the Virtues, a Palladian bridge, and a Gothic temple. William Kent even designed a temple dedicated to great Englishmen.

The designers of Castle Howard display a great love of cupolas, inspired by temple archi-tecture. The castle itself is topped by one that is extremely large for the period, and others feature on the Temple of the Four Winds and the Mausoleum. The landscape was seen as an opportunity not only to enchant the visitor, but also to enlighten him. In France, the gardens of Ermenonville and Méréville contain follies and pavilions that betray an interest in the same philosophical and historical themes—Newton's cenotaph, a column dedicated the explorer Captain Cook, the (real) tomb of Jean-Jacques Rousseau. Whether in France, Germany, or Britain, all of these gardens were designed as a reflection of the most progressive philosophies of their day.

Landscape garden of Wörlitz
J. Feyserbeck and
J.G. Schoch Neumark, 1765–1817,
Wörlitz, Germany

Stourhead
Henry Hoare and 1743,
Stourton, England

Stowe
William Kent and Capability Brown,
1713–1741, Buckingham, England

Above: A statue reclining
by the river in Wörlitz.
Right: The view over
the marshes from the stone
bridge in Stowe.
Following double spread: The
solid calm of the Pantheon in
Stourhead. Three visions of
peace and tranquillity.

Wörlitz, Stourhead, and other philosophical gardens

When Prince Franz von Anhalt-Dessau decided to begin work on his domain in Wörlitz in the eighteenth century, he was inspired by a philo-sophical ideal. What he planned was more than just a garden; it was to be a "garden-principality" measuring several square miles, and where he hoped to create an ideal society. The part of the river Elbe that crossed the domain was tamed with embankments, and a series of buildings were laid out in a philosophical walk. The prince's intellectual interests, typical of the Enlightenment, are reflected in the choice of buildings: a pantheon, temples to Venus and Flora, the Villa Hamilton (inspired by the home

Veitshöchheim

Veitshöchheim may not be among the best-known gardens in Europe, but it is certainly one of the most astonishing. It is a flamboyant rococo garden, built round the summer residence of the bishops of Würzburg. The castle itself is set among banks of flowers, while the nearby garden forms a maze of verdant spaces like individual rooms. The park was laid out in the mid-eighteenth century, and was conceived as a stage for the comedy of life, with the actors drawn from among the local nobility, who espoused the ideals of the Enlightenment. The idea of creating an experimental garden utopia was typical of the Enlightenment philosophy of looking to nature for symbols corresponding to human emotions and sentiments. Rationality was the key to a successful, serene life, while the popularity of pastoral themes in art was a reflection of a deep-rooted need to return to a simpler way of life in the bosom of nature. Themes from ancient Greek art and literature such as mythological creatures, Arcadian shepherds and shepherdesses, and other allegorical nature scenes were the source of this new sensibility which sprang from a belief in the perfectibility of mankind if society did not become too distanced from its roots in nature.

The walk takes us along shady paths between tall topiary hedges to the great lake and Mount Parnassus—in fact an extremely large pond. We climb the double staircase of the grotto pavilion, covered in carved shells, and, further on, we come across a Chinese pavilion, and nearby its Turkish counterpart, tucked away in the corner of a woodland grove. Everywhere we look are the delightful statues of the talented sculptor Ferdinand Tietz. They are dancing, a smile on their stone faces, a charming addition to the atmosphere of liberty that is so characteristic of this garden.

Saiho-ji
Muso Kokushi, 1334, Kyoto, Japan

It would take a lifetime to discover all the secrets of the many hundreds of gardens in Kyoto, such as Saiho-ji. In some ways, all are alike, but each is unique. Although nearly all are tiny, they create a vision of an infinite universe.

Saiho-ji and Japanese Miniatures

In Japan, gardens are a way of describing the world in miniature. Saiho-ji is a famous moss garden in the former imperial capital of Kyoto. In the upper garden, a cascade—designed to imitate a waterfall without actually using water—plunges down the hill into a frothy sea of moss. This astonishing, highly symbolic garden has served as a model for numerous other dry stone gardens over the centuries. In Daisein-in, in the Daitoku-ji group of temples, a river of white pebbles seems to flow down from Mount Horai, symbolized by topiary camellia shrubs. Ryogen-in temple has a similarly minimalist garden, where a slanting stone represents the cosmic mountain sacred to Buddhism. The artfully arranged stones often express powerful emotions.

Some Japanese gardens can be as simple as a stretch of raked sand with a heap of sand in the middle on which grows a tuft of grass. The infinite simplicity of the scene draws the observer into the heart of a universe of unexpected complexity. This traditional style of Japanese garden is still in vogue today, as shown by the garden of Shodo Suzuki or the extremely large garden at the Shimane art museum.

During the Edo period, in the early seventeenth century, the first Japanese gardens with walks were created. The visitor can stroll past the various *meisho*, or representations of famous scenery or landmarks. In Kumamoto, the garden of Joju-en stages a miniature Mount Fuji and even the Shinkansen, or bullet train linking Kyoto and Tokyo. The garden is on a grand scale, and is in fact closer in spirit to the Chinese style of the same period.

A return to intimacy

As the saying goes, an Englishman's home is his castle. In that case, the garden is the rampart that guarantees his privacy and protects him from unwanted intrusions from the world outside. This is true for private gardens the world over. In Japan, before entering a garden, there are certain formalities that have to be respected to preserve the tranquillity that reigns within: visitors must wait for a moment or two at the entrance to absorb the atmosphere of the home, drink some tea offered as a sign of welcome, tread softly on the damp ground, and bend their head to pass under a little curtain hanging in the doorway of the house itself. In a similar vein, in Europe, some gardens are designed as a series of separate "rooms." To pass from one to another is to cross the threshold between two different, but equally private, spaces. As a garden is an expression of the owner's personality, trespassing can be seen as the equivalent of a gratuitous insult.

The superb fortress of the Alhambra in Granada retains a sense
of intimacy thanks to the series of courtyards open to the sky.
Léon-Auguste Asselineau, *The Alberca Court in the Alhambra*,
lithograph, 1853, private collection.

The Jardin Flou

Collective of Catalan architects, 2002, Chaumont-sur-Loire, France

The combination of tulle curtains and white flowers give an impression of intimacy in this subtle garden devoted to the pleasure of the senses.

In 2002, the Garden Festival in Chaumont-sur-Loire hosted one of the most original garden designs since the creation of the show in 1993, on the theme of eroticism in the garden.

The designers were inspired by this theme to hang a dozen large sheets of white gauze on lines across their allotted space. There were openings in the veils, creating an infinitely varied play of views. Visitors disappeared and reappeared between the gauze sheets, a playful reference to erotic, tantalising glimpses of flesh as a lover undresses.

The gauzy maze is like a kaleidoscope of human desires. The play of veils and trasparency blurs and distorts the limits of the garden.

The plants chosen for this modern variation on the traditional theme of the white garden were all white, grey, or silvery green in color. These muted shades played an important part in creating an atmosphere of intimacy.

Seison-kaku

Prince Maeda, nineteenth century, Kanazawa, Japan

In Seison-kaku, the house merges into the garden, creating a subtle metaphor of man's place in nature.

Seison-kaku is characterised by the atmosphere of intimacy that reigns both inside the home and in the surrounding garden. It forms part of the much larger garden of Kenroku-En in the city of Kanazawa.

The home belonged to the widowed mother of the thirteenth feudal Lord Nariyasu of the Maeda clan. The tiny garden is hidden behind walls. A fast-flowing stream zigzags across the garden and into the house at one of the corners. The floor of the room set aside for the stream is made of roughly hewn stones.

The building, on two floors and with a cantilevered roof, stands right over the stream, with just one prop resting on a large rock supporting the roof. Stones were placed in the bed of the stream so that the elderly

widow could leave her home without getting her feet wet. Of all the gardens in Japan, this is the one where nature and society intermingle the most completely. The house is built, almost literally, on water, the very definition of transience. Yet it has survived nearly 150 years. It is impossible not to be touched by such a refined and delicate homage to man's intimate bond with nature.

Secret gardens

If an Englishman's home really is his castle,
then the garden is the moat. Once within his
own garden, he can turn his back on the hectic
world outside. The *Jardin Flou* in Chaumont-
sur-Loire was designed as just such a refuge, a
poetic place of retreat. Like Seison-kaku, half
a world away, it is a subtly ambiguous play
on the concepts of home and garden, interior
and exterior.

The Alhambra is refined to such a degree
that it could only be a private, secluded garden.
Ever detail is so luxurious that there can be no
reason to ever leave, other than to appreciate it
all the more on one's return.

La Fronteira is equally secluded, but for
reasons that seem to have more to do with
hiding certain things from prying eyes—family
secrets, jokes that can only be shared with close
friends and whose tastes one can be certain of.
The fashion for garden rooms in the early twentieth century reflects the move towards a more intimate, family-centered society. In the eighteenth
century, similar nooks were designed for lovers…
Today, garden rooms are designed with a sense
of narrative coherence in mind. Each space has
its own given theme—white flowers, roses, a
rockery, plants in terracotta pots. The fashion
spread from Great Britain all over the world.
But enclosed or walled gardens are nothing
new. As early as the Middle Ages, they were
seen as having a poetic, dream-like quality. The
medieval allegory of the Romaunt of the Rose,
set in a walled garden, is a notable example.
However, the philosophical and religious
dimension of the walled garden only became

apparent in the twentieth century. Grasping the significance of the private gardens of artists like Monet or Majorelle is a vital element in understanding their creative vision. They needed walls to be able to focus on their vision without distraction.

The same desire for intimacy is evident in many Oriental gardens. Chinese gardens often include mazes, while Japanese ones are often on a tiny scale—not to mention the art of bonsai, which truly brings the garden into the private, domestic sphere.

The famous rose bower and the white garden in Sissinghurst are justly famed and imitated the world over. Gardens based on a single color were a revolutionary new idea in the 1930s.

The Alhambra

Arriving in the vicinity of the fortress-palace, there is no hint of the superb gardens behind the walls. The Mexuar, Lindajara, and Reja patios, and the Courts of Myrtles and of Lions shimmer in the sun like a string of pearls. The majesty of the setting became apparent when I lifted my eyes to the Sierra Nevada mountains or towards Sacro-Monte. I felt quite insignificant surrounded by such magnificence. The stucco work and mosaics that decorate the walls add to the impression of intimacy and elegance—an impression created by the profusion of fountains, the water mirror, the group of small columns that furnish the Lion Court, and the water that trickles and splashes all around in channels and basins. Only the Daraxa garden is teeming with plants and birds. But the crowds of visitors have to a great extent killed the sense of hushed calm that once hung in the perfumed air. What would I give to be able to plunge into the heart of one of the eighteenth- or nineteenth-century engravings that show a private, intimate Alhambra, where the women sprawl at the foot of a pillar drinking tea, while their children play nearby. The delightful intimacy of the gardens has been largely lost due to architectural historians bent on highlighting the role of the Alhambra as a seat of power. In the process, the most charming aspect of the gardens has been neglected. Only very early in the morning can one still have a glimpse of the Alhambra when it was a home rather than a museum.

in a piece of cloth in the hands of the surgeon? On another tile, the doctor seems to be attending to his injured paw. Yet another shows a dog playing the trumpet, another playing the organ, and a third conducting a choir of two cats. In the art gallery on the chapel terrace, the themes depicted are less playful and more symbolic. A young woman is shown walking down a staircase accompanied by a handsome knight wearing a mask and wrapped in a cape, who is obviously trying to win the favors of his young companion. The benches on the same terrace are, for their part, decorated with erotic, not to say downright pornographic, scenes. It is difficult to think of another example of a garden which gives such an impression of trespassing on the privacy of the owner.

The meaning behind the tiles remains a mystery. The author Pascal Quignard was inspired by his interpretation of the tiles of Fronteira to write a novel: "They can be seen as an infinite, fantastic, topsy-turvy world, represented by animals, a world where humans seem lost in this crazy bestiary. This strange world is perfectly illustrated by certain *azulejos*, in particular some scenes that could be considered shocking on the benches on the chapel terrace, some hybrid characters, or the glances of complicity and nonchalant smiles on the exotic faces, the masks and grotesque figures that capture the attention of passers-by and invite them in to stroll through this dream world." *

* Pascal Quignard, *La Fronteira* (Paris: Chandeigne, 1992).

Fronteira

Fronteira
Marquis de Fronteira, 1668,
Benfica, Portugal

The gardens of Fronteira are richly decorated with *azulejos* and sculptures.

The baroque garden commissioned by the Marquis de Fronteira in Benfica, near Lisbon, manages to produce an impression of aristocratic pomp and circumstance and yet at the same time of great intimacy.

The palace is a magnificent sight, with its striking red façade that contrasts sharply with the blue *azulejos*—tiles—of the Gallery of Kings. Between the two there runs a parterre of topiary box hedges alternating with lead statues. But the pomp soon gives way to informality, as soon as you take a closer look at the *azulejos* that line the walls. The comical scenes depicted are far from regal. What sweet nothings are the two men whispering to the woman with a mask hiding her eyes? Why is the monkey farting into a trumpet? Why is someone pricking the boar's rump with a spear to make it walk? Why is the cat wrapped

Hidcote Manor gardens
Lawrence Johnson, 1907,
Hidcote Bartrim, England
Great Dixter
Gertrude Jekyll, Edwin Lutyens,
early twentieth century,
Northiam, England

In both Hidcote (facing page)
and Great Dixter (above), the
tall hedges create a series of
garden "rooms" open to the sky,
each with its own particular
theme.

Hidcote and other private gardens

In 1907, Major Lawrence Johnston began work on an unusual garden, at Hidcote Manor in the Cotswold hills. He settled on a design based on topiary hedges as a way of setting out the different themed areas he wanted to create. He knew it was important to mark the limits of each area clearly to avoid an incoherent mix of styles. The resulting design can be described as a sort of house open to the sky, where the visitor can walk from one room to another, and where each space fulfils a given role. From the very beginning, it was planned to use wooden trellises to separate the various areas. The trellises have long since been overgrown by the yew and hornbeam hedges. Immediately in front of the manor house is the great meadow, cut off by a yew hedge. Round the corner of the house is the white garden, a secret space where topiary pigeons stand guard over the flowerbeds. Next is the old garden, which affords a view of the red flowerbeds and the two brick gazebos, but the space is cut off by a gate. Perpendicular to this

view are two circular spaces that add to the feeling of intimacy. From there, the path leads on through massed banks of hydrangeas, along a stream lined with ferns, and on to the great walk—a lawn several hundred feet in length that leads down to an open gateway. This is the only point in the garden where the view is not cut off short by a hedge, although since the house stands on a slope, the plain below seems far distant. Did Major Johnston set out to create such a feeling of seclusion, or did he want to keep his outstanding collection of plants to himself?

The famous gardens at Sissinghurst share this atmosphere of other-worldly seclusion, heightened by the mellow brick walls that protect the Tudor mansion. The gardens were the work of Harold Nicholson and especially his wife Vita Sackville-West, who were good friends of Major Johnston. They wanted a garden designed along architectural lines. Vita Sackville-West wrote about her plans for a combination of long walks running north-south and east-west, with at the end of each an eye-catching feature, such as a statue, elegant Italian poplars, or a gateway. To the sides of each walk there would lie small, well-designed gardens, open to the sky, like the rooms of a house. She wanted as much freedom as possible to place the plants as she chose. The feeling of intimacy in the gardens at Sissinghurst arises from the outstanding choice of plants—you almost feel as if you are an uninvited guest at a select garden party—and in particular the

white garden, with its central rose bower, the essence of refined delicacy. The *Jardin Flou* at the Chaumont-sur-Loire Garden Festival had something of the same fragile magic.

The feeling of intimacy in the gardens of Great Dixter is of a different nature—maybe because the owner still works in the garden in a daily basis. Christopher Lloyd is somehow terribly British, with his muddy wellingtons and old jackets out at the elbow. He has imbued every plant in his garden with a piece of his soul. He is also an extremely popular garden writer, whose books on the subject are to be found on every amateur gardener's shelf. He specialiszes in flowered meadows, and is proud of the fact that he is not afraid to try out new, untested ideas. Visiting his garden, one gets a sense that here is a true amateur in the finest sense of the word—someone who has devoted his life to the garden he inherited from his parents. The gardens were designed by Gertrude Jekyll and Edwin Lutyens, the most celebrated architects and garden designers of the early twentieth century. The gardens at Great Dixter are a treasure trove of banks of flowers, meadows, orchards, octagonal ponds, and staircases. The atmosphere is modest— this is a family home, not a great palace—but the gardens are among the richest in Britain. Now nearly a century old, the design is as fresh as the day it was thought of. In this corner of the Sussex hills, time seems to have stood still since the fifteenth century when the cornerstone of the house was laid.

La Malbaie

La Malbaie, created in the 1950s by Francis
Cabot, lies on the banks of the Saint Lawrence
in Quebec. However, it was only in the 1980s
that Mr. Cabot really began to develop his
garden. Inspired by the examples of Hidcote
Manor and Sissinghurst, he turned the garden
into a series of rooms open to the sky. Among
the finest features are a circle of cedars and a yew
oval, a rose garden, a water staircase, and a series
of ponds. The dovecote is similar in design to
the gazebos at Hidcote. It stands at the far end
of a long water mirror, facing the surrounding
countryside across a lake. The white garden is

based on the one at Sissinghurst. The botanical
collections are one of the highlights of the
garden, which is especially impressive given the
climate in this corner of Canada. Winter lasts for
months on end and the plants mostly flower in a
very short period in July and August.
Paradoxically, the drifts of snow protect the

plants, and the garden awakens refreshed by its long sleep in spring, when the plants all come to life in the space of a few days. The most astonishing feature of La Malbaie is the ravine, similar to the one in Chaumont-sur-Loire. Both are dark and dank, with winding, narrow paths overhung with broad-leaved plants. Mr. Cabot likes to compare the atmosphere in the ravine with the hot, steamy jungle paintings by Henri Rousseau. Daring visitors can cross the ravine on the rope bridges to the little Japanese tea pavilion. It is hard to believe that we are still just a few miles from the bustling little Canadian town we left that morning.

Dumbarton Oaks

Dumbarton Oaks
Beatrice Farrand, 1921–1947,
Washington D.C., USA

The idea behind Dumbarton
Oaks, laid out in the first half
of the twentieth century, was to
prove that the Italian style
could be adapted to American
tastes. It was a great success.

The early twentieth century was a time of great prosperity for the United States. The time had come to develop an American garden tradition. Until then, only eighteenth-century gardens, such as the one at Williamsburg, had shown a spark of an original American style. The risk was that America would forever look to Europe for reference, as had happened with architecture. A group of influential friends, including the novelist Edith Wharton, set out to plead the cause of an independent American style, inspired by the refined Italian tradition. Dumbarton Oaks, in Washington, was one of the first gardens to be created as part of this new movement. It was laid out between 1921 and 1947 by Beatrice Farrand, an American landscape architect who was a keen exponent of William Robinson's theories and an admirer of Gertrude Jekyll's signature banks of flowers. The new American style was a subtle synthesis of several European influences, including the formal French and Italian garden layout and the British love of flowers. The water and gravel garden is reminiscent of French or Italian formal borders, with shades of Duchêne's water garden at Blenheim. The stone walls and buttresses have an American flavor, but the overall architecture is typically Italian. The double staircase, for example, is very Italian, but the choice of colors in the tulip and chrysanthemum borders are clearly inspired by Gertrude Jekyll's work. Dumbarton Oaks is the prototype for what in later decades became the East Coast style of garden design, found in countless private homes up and down the Atlantic seaboard. It has often been said that Dumbarton Oaks is the most intimate of all the great American public gardens.

Giverny

It might seem paradoxical to talk of the intimacy of such a world-famous garden as Giverny. It is true that given the hordes of visitors who descend on the garden and celebrated water-lily pond by the busload, it is hard to imagine the calm serenity that Claude Monet sought to create in this quiet corner of the Normandy countryside. It could also be said that the quality of light here is so bold and vibrant that it floods every corner, leaving no secret nooks where an atmosphere of intimacy might develop. Monet himself called this garden his masterpiece. He considered it no different from one his paintings, the result of a strong will and lots of hard work. One of his gardeners reported, "He wanted both tulips and roses, primroses and lupins. How could we do that? Nature could not obey his orders! He would have liked the banks of flowers to look exactly as he decided to paint them. Of course, he did love flowers, but his impatient, often irascible personality led him to demand that nature submit to his requirements, which was obviously impossible."

Giverny is a unique opportunity to reach the heart of a renowned artist's vision through his garden. Forget the crowds, focus on the superb irises or poppies, and call Monet's paintings before your mind's eye. Stroll along the central walkway, between the unruly nasturtium borders. Cross the Japanese bridge under a cloud of white wisteria. Between the verdant fronds of a weeping willow, watch the water sparkling round the water-lilies. This is the true Giverny.

Majorelle

This garden, on the outskirts of Marrakech, is a world in itself. Once you have passed the gate, you feel as if you could spend the rest of your life inside. It is an artist's garden, heavily influenced by Art Deco in the use of interweaving geometric shapes and striking colors such as reddish-brown, yellow, and a powerful, intense blue. The abundant vegetation adds a touch of acid green, while the geraniums glow pinkish-red. Bamboo groves grow alongside banks of papyrus, swaying gently in the breeze. The house is a cross between Art Deco and traditional Arabic styles, typical of colonial architecture from the dawn of the twentieth century. The walkways are simply paths of concrete painted red. The blue ponds, thickly scattered with water-lilies and duckweed, are surrounded with forests of cacti and jungles of agaves. The trees seem to huddle together to fit into the small space. It is true that the garden is tiny. The view along the canal can only be fully appreciated from a corner of the garden, through the Arab pavilion. Wherever you look, pink and red bougainvilleas cascade down the walls and pergolas, while a few palm trees tower high above the tops of the other trees. The ponds and fountains attract noisy flocks of birds that twitter constantly. The artist's eye who designed this garden wanted every plant, every detail, every refinement, to play a role in the impression made by the whole. The result is an intensely private, intimate space. If possible, it is best to visit the garden out of season, when the walkways are less thronged with crowds of tourists.

Majorelle
Louis Majorelle, 1920s,
Marrakech, Morocco

Majorelle is a tiny garden, but has room for several huge trees and a profusion of exotic plants. The colours are vibrant blues, yellows, and browns.

Suzhou

Suzhou
Designer unknown,
ninth and thirteenth centuries,
Suzhou, China

Suzhou: a maze of canals, high walls, and here and there, a glimpse of a magic, serene world through a window or doorway.

Like Venice, the Chinese city of Suzhou is built on water. But unlike Venice, where there are no gardens for the owners of the palaces to walk in, Suzhou is fortunate enough to boast magnificent gardens. These large, welcoming public spaces mean that in Suzhou, homes are very private, and it is a rare privilege to be invited over the threshold. The very names of the gardens are poetic: Garden of the Unsuccessful Politician, Garden of the Nonchalant Promenade, Garden of the Master of Fishing Nets, or Garden of Pleasure. In the grounds of each garden are numerous pavilions, complicated rock gardens, and abundant botanical collections. Although the atmosphere is one of great intimacy, the aim of the garden design is to encapsulate the local scenery and produce an image of the landscape that creates the illusion of space. The intertwining streams, the ponds strung together like beads, the buildings that seem to merge into each other, and the luxuriant vegetation together create an ambience of mystery and seclusion that no Western garden can hope to imitate. Our landscape architects could learn a great deal by studying the thinking behind the great Chinese public gardens.

Gardens for the people

Back in the eighteenth century, before the French Revolution ushered in a more democratic era, public gardens were few and far between in Europe. Their existence depended on the goodwill of the monarch towards his subjects. In France, the first public gardens were set up in the private parks seized from the nobility during the Revolution. In Britain, the Victorian period was the golden era for great public works, such as the Crystal Palace built for the Great Exhibition in 1851.

Nowadays, public parks depend on the generosity of councils and local authorities rather than the largesse of monarchs or aristocrats. Rather than being an optional extra, parks and gardens are now planned right from the conception of an architectural project—the Garden Cities built after the Second World War to re-house countless bombed-out families were an important recognition of the role of the garden in creating a new, forward-looking society.

John Bachman, *Central Park, Summer. Looking South*, 1865,
lithograph, Museum of the City of New York, USA.

Central Park

Frederick Law Olmsted, 1858, New York, USA

Its sheer size and the range of activities makes Central Park the playground of the New Yorkers and one of the highlights of a trip to the city.

It is often said that if Central Park is so unfailingly popular with New Yorkers, it is because it was not planned by a landscape architect interested only in the formal beauty of the design, but by someone who actually cared about the wants and needs of the people who would be using the park every day. The park was the brainchild of Frederick Law Olmsted, who in 1857 came up with the idea of a 840-acre (340-hectare) park right in the heart of the city. He chose a vast stretch of unused land, a traditional meeting place for Algonquin Indians, who gathered round a large sloping stone there as late as the eighteenth century. It took fifteen years to plant the five hundred thousand trees in the park. But finally, Olmsted's dream of a place of relaxation for all New Yorkers to share was realized.

The incredible diversity of the landscape and the sheer size of the park are unparalleled. There are half a dozen small lakes, and one gigantic reservoir, hills, formal gardens, rose gardens, fruit orchards, meadows, sports grounds, a skating rink, museums, an imitation medieval castle, a petting zoo, a planetarium, and the Bethesda fountain. After John Lennon's tragic death, his widow Yoko Ono made a gift of hundreds of trees to the park's Strawberry Fields in his memory. The

park is always full of surprises. What makes Central Park such a wonderful place is its endless diversity. Whether you want to whiz

round on the latest rollerblades, ride in a horse-drawn carriage, or simply soak up the sun by one of the lakes, Central Park has something for you. Today, New York would be unthinkable without the green heart that beats at its center.

Nîmes la Fontaine

Jacques-Philippe Maréchal, 1745–1760, Nîmes, France

The strictly classical grounds of the Jardin de la Fontaine include an unparalleled collection of baroque sculptures by the finest French artists of the eighteenth century.

The Jardin de la Fontaine in the southern French city of Nîmes was founded in the eighteenth century. The name comes from a Roman fountain in the grounds. Its creation was ordered by King Louis XV, who wanted a garden to his own glory—and the park is fittingly majestic. The numerous double staircases, balusters, sculpted stone urns, and magnificent statues are all symbols of the monarch's absolute power. The garden begins at the top of the hill, where the Roman tower called the Tour Magne provides a lookout post over whole city and the surrounding countryside. Walks and staircases lead down the hill towards the city. The lower part of the garden is planted with nettle trees, plane trees, chestnut trees, and linden trees. A canal flows across the park. Water is everywhere, in the form of ponds and trickling streams, cooling the air. The early twentieth century writer Colette wrote a beautiful description of the gardens: "The baths of Diana that I am leaning over reflect, always and forever, Judas trees, terebinth trees, pines, mauve-flowered paulownias [...] A whole garden of reflections is turned upside-down below me, and mixed in the water, turns from aquamarine to dark blue, the purple of a bruised peach, the brown of dried blood [...] The beautiful garden, the beautiful silence, where the only sound is the thrumming of the imperious, green, transparent, dark water, blue and shiny like a lively dragon." *

* Colette, *La Naissance du Jour* (Paris: Flammarion, 1984).

Gardens of their time

Facing page: The Jardin du Luxembourg, designed by Boyceau de la Bareaudière, is the archetypal French garden, with manicured lawns and an abundance of marble statues. It is extremely popular with Parisians of all ages.

Below: The Prater was once a royal hunting ground, which Emperor Joseph II opened to his subjects in 1766. The famous Ferris wheel was installed in 1896.

Why, in the twenty-first century, when fruit and vegetables come from the supermarket and flowers are delivered wrapped in cellophane, do so many people still feel the urge to grow their own plants—even if it is just in a pot on a sunny windowsill? Maybe it is because plants are so truly alive. It is thrilling to watch a tendril reaching out and curling round a bamboo cane. And so while the great modern gardens are no longer commissioned by princes, but by mayors, one aspect of garden design has remained constant: it has always been adapted to the demands of the society of the day. Central Park, for instance, was the brainchild of a journalist who foresaw the need for green spaces amid the great urban sprawl that New York was destined to become. The Jardin de la Fontaine in Nîmes was commissioned by a king who wanted to win over his reluctant subjects,

and so offered them a garden in accordance with their tastes. Modern gardens on old industrial sites, such as Gas Work Park in Seattle, reflect contemporary concerns with environmental issues and hark back to a gentler, less industrialized society. In fact, this was already the case in the mid-nineteenth century with the Buttes Chaumont in Paris, which was explicitly planned to give the poorer quarters of Paris somewhere healthy to spend their leisure time.

Much of this book relates the grandiloquent plans of kings and princes. Some monarchs did have the best interests of their subjects at heart. Emperor Joseph II made a gift of one of his hunting reserves to the people of Vienna. It became the Prater fairground. Ritsurin in Japan, which originally belonged to the ruling Ikoma family, was also gifted to the people in 1873.

Ever since the first towns sprang up, men have always striven to combine urban life with a deep-rooted need for greenery and open spaces. Garden towns and cities such as Welwyn in England or Le Vésinet near Paris were, in their day, visionary attempts to unite town and country.

Of course, gardens are inherently fragile—a few years of neglect, and they return to the wild. But maybe this is why even modern societies still feel the need to create new gardens: it is a way of acknowledging that deep down, we know that we are totally dependent on our environment for our quality of life.

Gas Work Park
Richard Haag, 1972, Seattle, USA

Gas Work Park opened the way for numerous projects designed to restore polluted wastelands while not turning our backs on our industrial heritage.

Gas Work Park

Industrial wastelands have become a familiar feature of our urban landscape. In the past, these were ugly eyesores, but nowadays, more and more landscape architects are seeing them as an interesting challenge—how to create a beautiful public park out of a derelict stretch of scrub grass.

In 1971, the landscape architect Richard Haag was commissioned to create a public park on the shores of Lake Union on the site of an abandoned gasworks. He came up with an audacious plan: given the spectacular hulk of the ruin, he decided to plan the park around it. He compared the rough beauty of the site to the Eiffel Tower, and set out to "renovate" the metal structure and pipes. The plan was not to prettify the site by disguising its industrial heritage, but rather make a feature of it, even keeping the rust patches. Only a few elements were repainted in bright colors, to balance the structure or to distinguish the children's play areas. The grounds were depolluted before great meadows were laid out, where the people of Seattle could enjoy flying kites or cycling. A huge sundial, made of industrial waste such as broken fragments of ceramic, bitumen, and iron foundry offcasts, stands on a small bluff.

This park may seem a radical new departure in garden design, but it is in fact in the finest tradition of garden history. The fascination with the skeleton of an industrial installation is reminiscent of the eighteenth-century love of Gothic ruins and follies. Nor is the idea of recycling materials new. The floor mosaics in the

classical garden of Collodi, near Pistoia, Italy, are also made of foundry offcasts.

This is not to detract from the originality of Richard Haag's plan. He was the first to see the landscaping potential of such industrial sites, and his ideas have been borrowed in many parts of the world. The heavily industrialized Ruhr valley in Germany is a good example. In Duisburg, Peter Latz designed a garden round a vast steelworks, planting birch, ash, and aspen as well as a garden of weeds. The garden has a magical atmosphere of poetic abandon.

The Buttes Chaumont

The Buttes Chaumont gardens, in the east of Paris, were founded in 1867 in an old gypsum quarry that had previously been used as a rubbish dump and a knacker's yard. It was not an attractive site. In order to save money, the gardens' designers, Alphand and Barillet Deschamps, used rubble to build up small hills, creating rocky, almost lunar landscapes, using the sides of the quarry to stage plunging precipices. The upper part of the quarry became an alpine meadow, and in the bottom of the valley was a lake. The designers took special care with the most beautiful panoramas. On the cliff stands a small temple. A network of paths weaves through the park. It is a pleasant place to while away a sunny afternoon getting lost in the meanders of the walks before returning to the busy hum of the city.

The Buttes Chaumont gardens were originally designed as the lungs of Paris, which was terribly polluted by coal smoke throughout the nineteenth century. The gardens are similar in conception to the great designs of the Enlightenment, such as the landscaping of the Ilm valley near Weimar, undertaken by the great German poet Johann Wolfgang von Goethe. The architects charged with designing the Buttes Chaumont set out to turn a blight on the Paris landscape into a place of pleasure and relaxation for the city's poorest inhabitants. It is truly sublime in the original meaning of the word, where beauty is tinged with a sense of awe and even fear at the majesty of the landscape.

Ritsurin

Ritsurin is a calm, tranquil park. But this is exactly what makes it such a haven in the go-getting city of Takamatsu, where the local authorities have announced their ambition of building the most overpasses of any city in Japan—although the example of Tokyo shows that such viaducts are a real eyesore. Ritsurin is a magical place, nestled on the gently sloping flanks of a mountain covered in forest. It has six lakes and more than ten hills. In the eighteenth century, the local nobility was famed for its wealth and refinement. The tea pavilion on the lake, the great red bridge, the maples that turn a rich, burnished gold in autumn and the frothy pink of the cherry blossom in springtime, the avenue of mulberry trees trimmed like poodles—everything is perfect. It is a million miles from the bustle of the city.

Ritsurin
The Ikoma family, eighteenth century (restored in 1953), Takamatsu, Japan

Lying at the foot of a steep hill, Ritsurin has been an oasis of calm in the heart of the bustling city of Takamatsu since the eighteenth century.

Gaudi and the Guell park

Any park designed by Gaudi had to be an instant classic. Today this goes without saying, but it must be remembered that this most popular of parks was originally planned as a private real estate project. Where architects like Barragan and Burle-Marx designed fabulous gardens for the private enjoyment of a well-heeled few, the secret of the Guell park's popular success is in fact its failure—to attract any wealthy purchasers. Apart from the entrance pavilions, none of the lots were sold simply because the design was too audacious for the tastes of the conservative Spanish Catholic families.

The timidity of the wealthy Barcelona investors means that we are free to sit and dream on the immense terrace, or beneath the columns decorated with mosaic, to admire the lizard's head that spouts water from its mouth at the bottom of the water staircase, and to pay homage to the imagination of the architect who designed the slanting pillars of the upper terraces.

Gaudi's work distils the essence of European culture, combining Italian influences, a touch of Spanish eccentricity, and a restraining hint of French rationalism. It is fortunate indeed for us that the wealthiest families in Barcelona were not as far-sighted as the great architect.

Guell Park
Antonio Gaudi, 1900,
Barcelona, Spain

The Guell park in Barcelona is an example of a thoughtful housing development, where the space is cleverly used and richly decorated. The homes did not sell, but fortunately, the park remains open.

Le Vésinet and other garden cities

Le Vésinet
Paul-Bernard de Choulot, 1858,
Le Vésinet, France

A stream winds its way between the gardens, a lake, manicured lawns, and venerable old trees. The wealthy inhabitants of Le Vésinet live in a truly splendid setting. This is probably the most elegant and exclusive garden development anywhere in the world.

In 1856, the Duc de Morny, a wealthy French aristocrat, suggested the creation of a holiday village on a site measurin 1,112 acres (450 hectares some ten miles west of Paris, chosen because it was crossed by the first French railway line. The park was duly bought and divided into lots to a plan by the Comte de Choulot—another aristocrat—and a team of architects and engineers. By 1875, 1,500 people lived in Le Vésinet. Even today, the population is still under 20,000. In fact, it is really more of a gigantic garden dotted with villas than a town. Pleasant walks wind between the magnificent old trees and the superb private villas. The Comte de Choulot saw his pet project as fulfilling an explicitly political role, writing "to aggrandise art is to contribute to the progress of intelligence, to add the exquisite yet indefinable sensations of beauty to the pleasures of the spirit. It is to force the tastes of the nations to become so intimately linked that they blend together." He saw gardens as the perfect way of guaranteeing social harmony and defending the prevailing moral order: "so magnificently reduced by Le Nôtre to the art of decoration, [garden design] tends these days to come closer to the grandiose proportions of nature... So under its reign, the whole country... gives the image of perfect harmony."*

Le Vésinet was one of the earliest examples of what was to become known as the garden city. At about the same time, Olmsted founded Riverside, near Chicago. In Britain, Joseph Paxton founded Birkenhead, near Liverpool. It was another fifty years before the movement became widespread, with the creation of towns like Letchworth, Hampstead, and Welwyn Garden City in Britain, Teutoburgia and Margarethenhöhe in Germany, and Chatenay-Malabry in France. These new towns all promoted a dream of how society should be, best illustrated by an advertising leaflet for the new homes in Welwyn Garden City. Contented housewives push prams along the streets past old farm buildings that stand cheek by jowl with brand new maisonettes, and well-stocked shops. The garden city promised a vision of a friendly, egalitarian society that is a direct descendant of Thomas More's dream of Utopia.

* Quoted in Caroline Stefulesco's *L'Urbanisme Végétal* (Paris: IDF, 1993).

Index of gardens, places, and designers

Index of architects and garden designers

Photographic credits

ASK Images: pages 38 (M. Spencer), 86–87 (C. Thibault), 104–105 (A. Olszak), 134–135 (T. Anzenbergerr), 219 (R. Salzedo).

Ch. Bastin and J. Evrard: page 147.

Bildarchiv Monheim: pages 72–73, 150, 151, 173 (F. Monheim), 74–75 (A. Bednorz), 103 (M. Bassler), 107 (Monheim/Von Götz).

Bridgeman-Giraudon: pages 8 (Alinari), 34, 56, 88 (The Stapleton Collection), 118, 138, 160, 178 (The Stapleton Collection), 204.

P. Broquet: pages 16, 76, 78, 78–79, 124–125, 130–131, 142–143, 144–145, 152, 153, 166–167, 168, 172.

F. Caruncho: pages 32 top and bottom, 32–33.

CIPJP: page 134.

P. Davenport: page 162.

P. Delance: page 199.

Dia Center for the Arts/J. Cliett: pages 36, 37.

Digital vision: pages 42–43 (M. Colomb).

P. Estersohn: pages 5 top, 95.

F. Frankel: pages 18, 212, 213.

Getty images: pages 62–63 (H. Lloyd), 206–207 (M. Funk).

M. Greenhalgh: pages 162–163.

F. Grehan: page 115.

J. Habersetzer: pages 30, 31.

J. Harpur: pages 90, 91, 92–93.

HOA-QUI: pages 46–47 top (C. Vaisse), 50 top, 101, (W. Buss), 53 (P. Le Floch), 66 (C. Boissieux), 82–83 (J.-P. Lescourret), 84 top (A. Wolf), 102 (Ph. Renault), 104 (P. de Wilde), 176–177 (Martel), 188-189 (P. Delance).

Ch. Jencks: page 94.

Lamontagne: pages 15, 17, 20, 26-27, 58, 59, 60, 74, 97, 106, 108, 109, 128, 131, 140, 141 top and bottom, 146, 154, 184–185, 191, 192, 193, 196, 197, 202, 203, 215.

MAP: pages 40–41, 211, 214 (Y. Monel), 54, 55, 132, 136 bottom, 137, 155, 159 (N. et P. Mioulane), 128–129 (C. Nichols), 158 (F. Didillon).

G. Meguerdichiam: page 5 bottom.

Y. Monel: pages 5 middle, 180, 181, 220, 221.

V. Motte: pages 28, 51, 68, 69, 84 bottom, 110, 111, 198, 208–209.

C. Nichols: pages 133, 148–149, 149, 170–171.

PHOTONONSTOP: pages 24–25, 200 (X. Richer), 46 (Sime), 46–47 bottom (J.-C. Pratt), 136 top (A.G.E. Fotostock), 164–165 (Simeone), 201 (Y. Travert), 210 (D. Ball), 216, 217 (Jonathan), 218 (R. Mazin).

B. Pichon-Clarisse: pages 28–29.

J.-P. Pigeat: pages 6–7, 19, 23, 44–45, 48, 50 bottom, 80, 81, 98, 99, 100, 112 top and bottom, 113, 116, 117, 126 top and bottom, 126–127, 194 top and bottom, 195.

A. Reeve: page 163.

Le Scanff-Mayer: pages 10, 11, 12–13, 21, 52, 67, 71, 187.

D. Von Schaewen: pages 70, 120, 121, 157.

Seison kaku: pages 182, 182–183, 183.

Fotot Sulzer / Schlossverwaltung Hellbrunn : pages 122, 122–123.

TOP/RAPHO: pages 39, 85 (Jarry/Tripelon), 49, 174, 175 (F. Huguier), 64–65 (J. Sierpinski), 76–77 (J.-N. Reichel), 156 (K. Hart), 169 (R. Beaufré), 186 (H. Champollion), 190 (P. Hinous).

M. Viard/Horizon: page 114.